Contents

Nonfiction Reading Practice Is Important

Research indicates that more than 80 percent of what people read and write is nonfiction text. Newspapers, magazines, directions on new products, application forms, and how-to manuals are just some of the types of nonfiction reading material we encounter on a daily basis. As students move through the grades, an increasing amount of time is spent reading expository text for subjects such as science and social studies. Most reading comprehension sections on state and national tests are nonfiction.

Each Unit Has...

A Teacher Resource Page

Vocabulary words for all three levels are given. The vocabulary lists include proper nouns and content-specific words, as well as other challenging words.

A Visual Aid

The visual aid represents the topic for the unit. It is intended to build interest in the topic. Reproduce the visual on an overhead transparency or photocopy it for each student.

Articles at Three Reading Levels

Each unit presents three articles on the same topic. The articles progress in difficulty from easiest (Level 1) to hardest (Level 3). An icon indicates the level of the article—Level 1 (■), Level 2 (■ ■), Level 3 (■ ■ ■). Each article contains new vocabulary and ideas to incorporate into classroom discussion. The Level 1 article gives readers a core vocabulary and a basic understanding of the topic. More challenging vocabulary words are used as the level of the article increases. Interesting details also change or increase in the Levels 2 and 3 articles.

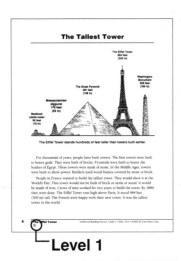

Level 1

Level 2

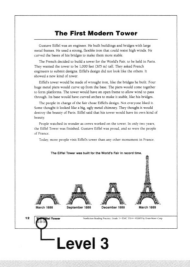

Level 3

Readability

All of the articles in this series have been edited for readability. Readability formulas, which are mathematical calculations, are considered to be one way of predicting reading ease. The Flesch-Kincaid and Fry Graph formulas were used to check for readability. These formulas count and factor in three variables: the number of words, syllables, and sentences in a passage to determine the reading level. When appropriate, proper nouns and content-specific terms were discounted in determining readability levels for the articles in this book.

Student Comprehension Pages

A vocabulary/comprehension page follows each article. There are five multiple-choice questions that provide practice with the types of questions that are generally used on standardized reading tests. The bonus question is intended to elicit higher-level thinking skills.

Level 1

Level 2

Level 3

Additional Resources

Six graphic organizers to extend comprehension are also included in the book. (See page 4 for suggested uses.)

Famous Person

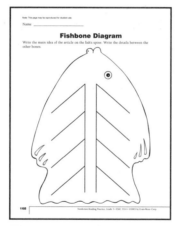

Fishbone Diagram

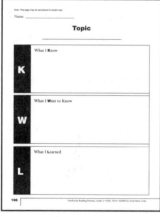

KWL Chart

Sequence Chart

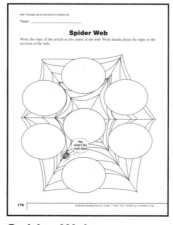

Spider Web

Word Quilt

How to Use *Nonfiction Reading Practice*

Planning Guided Reading Instruction

The units in this book do not need to be taught in sequential order. Choose the units that align with your curriculum or with student interests.

- For whole-group instruction, introduce the unit to the total class. Provide each student with an article at the appropriate reading level. Guide students as they read the articles. You may want to have students read with partners. Then conduct a class discussion to share the different information learned.

- For small-group instruction, choose an article at the appropriate reading level for each group. The group reads the article with teacher guidance and discusses the information presented.

- The articles may also be used to assist readers in moving from less difficult to more challenging reading material. After building vocabulary and familiarity with the topic at the appropriate level, students may be able to successfully read the article at the next level of difficulty.

Presenting a Unit

1. Before reading the articles, make an overhead transparency of the visual aid or reproduce it for individual student use. Use the visual to engage student interest in the topic, present vocabulary, and build background that will aid in comprehension. This step is especially important for visual learners.

2. Present vocabulary that may be difficult to decode or understand. A list of suggested vocabulary words for each article is given on the teacher resource page. Where possible, connect these words to the visual aid.

3. Present and model several appropriate reading strategies that aid in comprehension of the expository text. You may wish to make an overhead transparency of the reading strategies checklist on page 5 or reproduce it for students to refer to as they read.

4. You may want to use one of the graphic organizers provided on pages 166–171. Make an overhead transparency, copy the organizer onto the board or chart paper, or reproduce it for students. Record information learned to help students process and organize the information.

5. Depending on the ability levels of the students, the comprehension/vocabulary pages may be completed as a group or as independent practice. It is always advantageous to share and discuss answers as a group so that students correct misconceptions. An answer key is provided at the back of this book.

Name _____

Reading Checklist

Directions: Check off the reading hints that you use to understand the story.

Before I Read

_____ I think about what I already know.

_____ I think about what I want to learn.

_____ I predict what is going to happen.

_____ I read the title for clues.

_____ I look at the pictures for clues.

While I Read

_____ I stop and retell to check what I remember.

_____ I reread parts that are confusing.

_____ I read the captions under the pictures.

_____ I make pictures of the story in my mind.

_____ I figure out ways to understand hard words.

After I Read

_____ I think about what I have just read.

_____ I speak, draw, and write about what I read.

_____ I reread favorite parts.

_____ I reread to find details.

_____ I look back at the story to find answers to questions.

The Eiffel Tower

Introducing the Topic

1. Reproduce page 7 for individual students, or make a transparency to use with a group or your whole class.

2. Present the diagram of the tower, and read the caption and labels to connect the new vocabulary with a graphic representation.

Reading the Selection

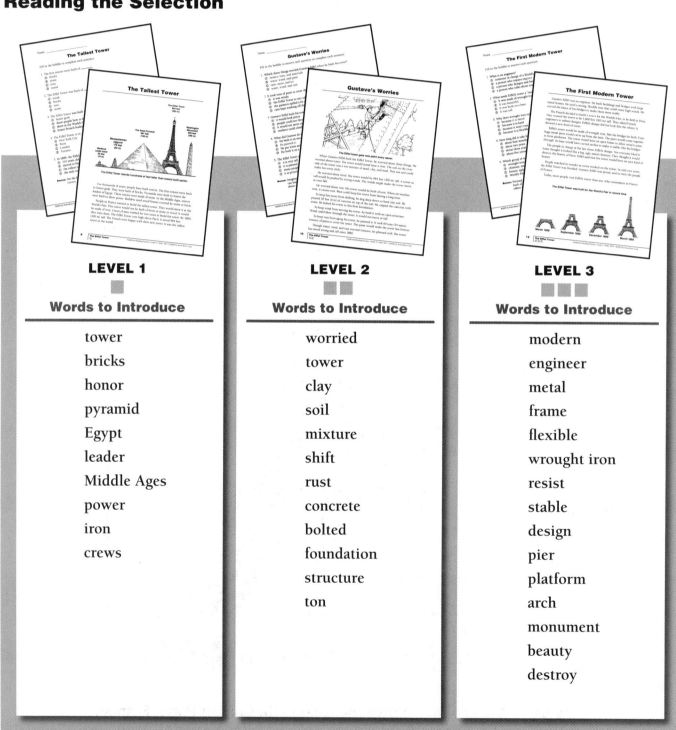

LEVEL 1

■

Words to Introduce

tower

bricks

honor

pyramid

Egypt

leader

Middle Ages

power

iron

crews

LEVEL 2

■ ■

Words to Introduce

worried

tower

clay

soil

mixture

shift

rust

concrete

bolted

foundation

structure

ton

LEVEL 3

■ ■ ■

Words to Introduce

modern

engineer

metal

frame

flexible

wrought iron

resist

stable

design

pier

platform

arch

monument

beauty

destroy

The Eiffel Tower

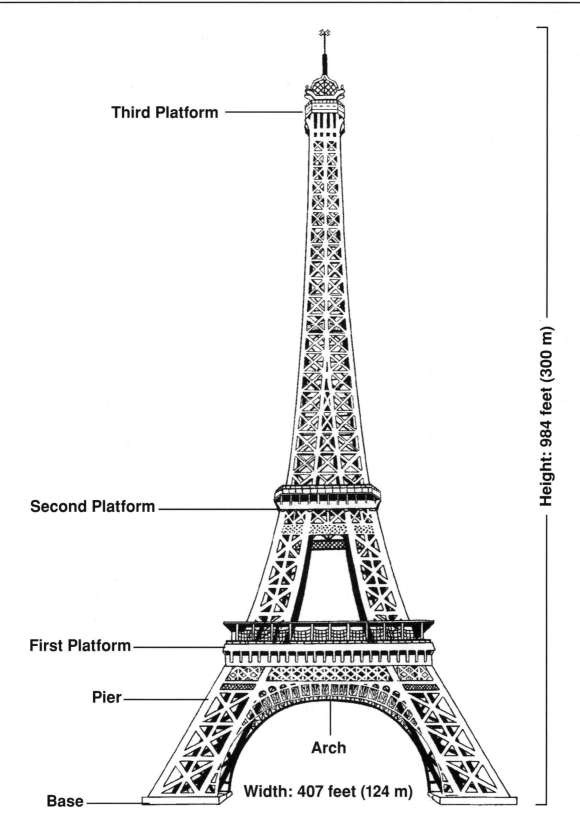

Third Platform

Second Platform

First Platform

Pier

Arch

Base

Height: 984 feet (300 m)

Width: 407 feet (124 m)

The Eiffel Tower soars above the Champ de Mars in Paris, France.

The Tallest Tower

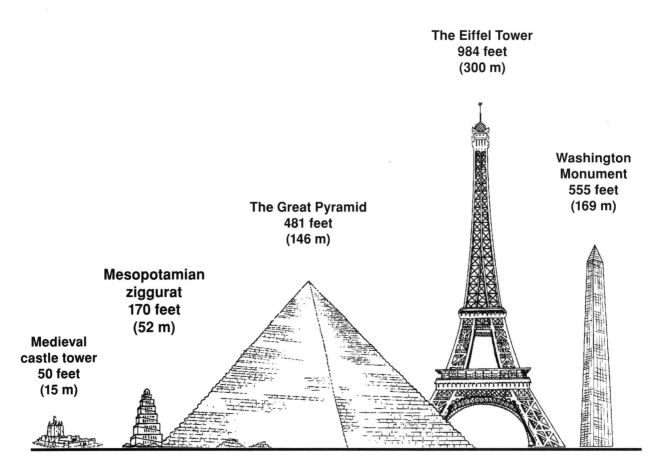

The Eiffel Tower stands hundreds of feet taller than towers built earlier.

For thousands of years, people have built towers. The first towers were built to honor gods. They were built of bricks. Pyramids were built to honor the leaders of Egypt. These towers were made of stone. In the Middle Ages, towers were built to show power. Builders used wood frames covered by stone or brick.

People in France wanted to build the tallest tower. They would show it at the World's Fair. This tower would not be built of brick or stone or wood. It would be made of iron. Crews of men worked for two years to build the tower. By 1889, they were done. The Eiffel Tower rose high above Paris. It stood 984 feet (300 m) tall. The French were happy with their new tower. It was the tallest tower in the world.

Name _____

The Tallest Tower

Fill in the bubble to complete each sentence.

1. The first towers were built of _____.
   - Ⓐ bricks
   - Ⓑ stone
   - Ⓒ iron
   - Ⓓ wood

2. The Eiffel Tower was built of _____.
   - Ⓐ wood
   - Ⓑ bricks
   - Ⓒ iron
   - Ⓓ stone

3. The Eiffel Tower was built to _____.
   - Ⓐ honor gods
   - Ⓑ show people how to build a tower
   - Ⓒ show at the World's Fair
   - Ⓓ honor French leaders

4. The Eiffel Tower is in _____.
   - Ⓐ New York City
   - Ⓑ Paris
   - Ⓒ London
   - Ⓓ Toronto

5. In 1889, the Eiffel Tower was _____.
   - Ⓐ 100 years old
   - Ⓑ moved to England
   - Ⓒ the tallest tower in the world
   - Ⓓ the only tower in the world

Bonus: On the back of this page, write some things that you learned about towers.

Gustave's Worries

The Eiffel Tower gets new paint every seven years.

When Gustave Eiffel built the Eiffel Tower, he worried about three things. He worried about water. The tower would stand near a river. The soil on the river side of the tower was a wet mixture of sand, clay, and mud. This wet soil could make his tower shift.

He worried about wind. His tower would be 984 feet (300 m) tall. A tower so tall would be pushed by strong winds. The winds might make the tower move, or even fall.

He worried about rust. His tower would be built of iron. When air touches iron, it causes rust. Rust could keep his tower from lasting a long time.

To keep his tower from shifting, he dug deep down to hard clay soil. He poured 20 feet (6 m) of concrete on top of the soil. He capped the concrete with stone. He bolted his tower to this firm foundation.

To keep wind from moving his tower, he built it with an open structure. Wind could blow through the tower. It would not move or fall.

To keep rust from aging his tower, he painted it. It took 60 tons (54 metric tonnes) of paint to cover the tower. The paint would make the tower last forever.

Although water, wind, and rust worried Gustave, he planned well. His tower has stood strong and tall since 1889.

Nonfiction Reading Practice, Grade 3 • EMC 3314 • ©2003 by Evan-Moor Corp.

Name _____

Gustave's Worries

Fill in the bubble to answer each question or complete each sentence.

1. Which three things worried Gustave Eiffel when he built his tower?
   - Ⓐ money, time, and materials
   - Ⓑ water, wind, and paint
   - Ⓒ rain, snow, and ice
   - Ⓓ water, wind, and rust

2. It took tons of paint to cover the Eiffel Tower because _____.
   - Ⓐ it was windy
   - Ⓑ the Eiffel Tower is very tall
   - Ⓒ the painters spilled a lot of paint
   - Ⓓ rain kept washing off the paint

3. Gustave Eiffel built his tower with an open structure so that _____.
   - Ⓐ it would look pretty
   - Ⓑ people could see through it
   - Ⓒ it would not move or fall
   - Ⓓ workers could climb on it

4. What did Gustave do to keep his tower from shifting?
   - Ⓐ He built it on wet soil.
   - Ⓑ He painted it.
   - Ⓒ He put wires around it.
   - Ⓓ He built it on a foundation of hard soil, concrete, and stone.

5. The Eiffel Tower will last a long time because _____.
   - Ⓐ it is very tall
   - Ⓑ it is painted to keep it from rusting
   - Ⓒ many people visit it
   - Ⓓ it is protected from the wind

Bonus: Imagine that you have been asked to build the world's tallest tower. You can build it anywhere in the world. On the back of this page, write about where you would build it and why.

The First Modern Tower

Gustave Eiffel was an engineer. He built buildings and bridges with large metal frames. He used a strong, flexible iron that could resist high winds. He curved the bases of his bridges to make them more stable.

The French decided to build a tower for the World's Fair, to be held in Paris. They wanted the tower to be 1,000 feet (305 m) tall. They asked French engineers to submit designs. Eiffel's design did not look like the others. It showed a new kind of tower.

Eiffel's tower would be made of wrought iron, like the bridges he built. Four huge metal piers would curve up from the base. The piers would come together to form platforms. The tower would have an open frame to allow wind to pass through. Its base would have curved arches to make it stable, like his bridges.

The people in charge of the fair chose Eiffel's design. Not everyone liked it. Some thought it looked like a big, ugly metal chimney. They thought it would destroy the beauty of Paris. Eiffel said that his tower would have its own kind of beauty.

People watched in wonder as crews worked on the tower. In only two years, the Eiffel Tower was finished. Gustave Eiffel was proud, and so were the people of France.

Today, more people visit Eiffel's tower than any other monument in France.

The Eiffel Tower was built for the World's Fair in record time.

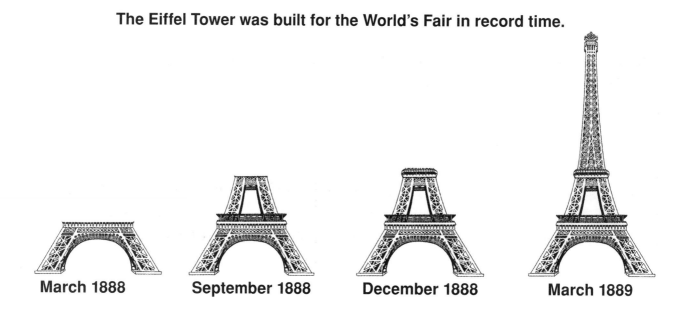

March 1888   **September 1888**   **December 1888**   **March 1889**

Name _____

The First Modern Tower

Fill in the bubble to answer each question.

1. What is an **engineer**?
   - Ⓐ someone in charge of a World's Fair
   - Ⓑ a person who repairs engines
   - Ⓒ a person who designs and builds things
   - Ⓓ a person who talks about towers

2. What made Eiffel's tower a "new kind of tower"?
   - Ⓐ It was made of wrought iron.
   - Ⓑ It was beautiful.
   - Ⓒ It was built on a base.
   - Ⓓ It was tall.

3. Why does wrought iron resist wind?
   - Ⓐ because it is metal
   - Ⓑ because it is hard
   - Ⓒ because it won't rust
   - Ⓓ because it is flexible

4. How long did it take for the Eiffel Tower to be completed?
   - Ⓐ about four months
   - Ⓑ about two years
   - Ⓒ about three years
   - Ⓓ about five years

5. Which group of words relate to what made the Eiffel Tower different?
   - Ⓐ wrought iron, arches, platforms
   - Ⓑ chimney, metal, monument
   - Ⓒ beauty, ugly, destroy
   - Ⓓ World's Fair, Paris, bridges

Bonus: Pretend that you lived in France when Eiffel's tower was built. On the back of this page, write a letter to the editor of the *Paris News*. Tell the editor what you think about Eiffel's design for the tower.

No More King!

Introducing the Topic

1. Reproduce page 15 for individual students, or make a transparency to use with a group or your whole class.

2. Present the map of the thirteen colonies, and read the caption and labels to connect the new vocabulary with a graphic representation.

Reading the Selection

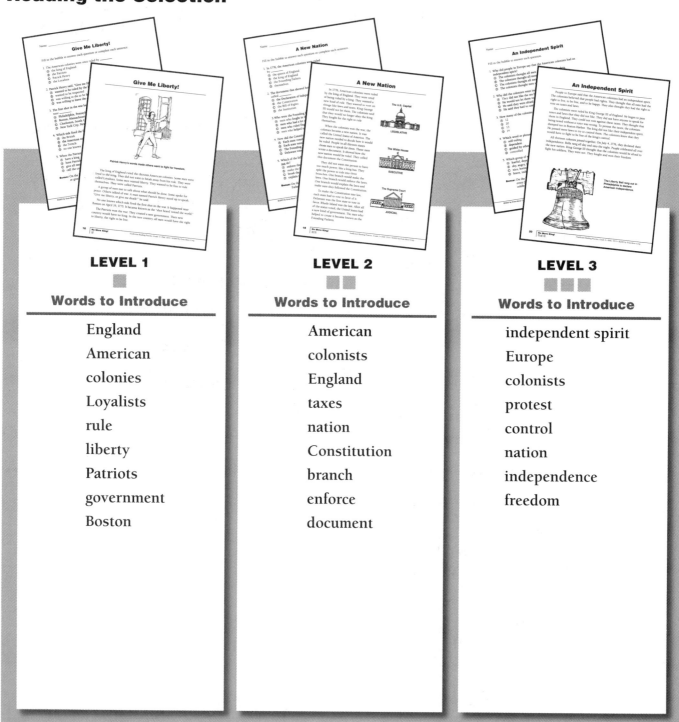

LEVEL 1	LEVEL 2	LEVEL 3
Words to Introduce	**Words to Introduce**	**Words to Introduce**
England	American	independent spirit
American	colonists	Europe
colonies	England	colonists
Loyalists	taxes	protest
rule	nation	control
liberty	Constitution	nation
Patriots	branch	independence
government	enforce	freedom
Boston	document	

Thirteen Original Colonies

In 1775, the thirteen American colonies were ruled by the British king.

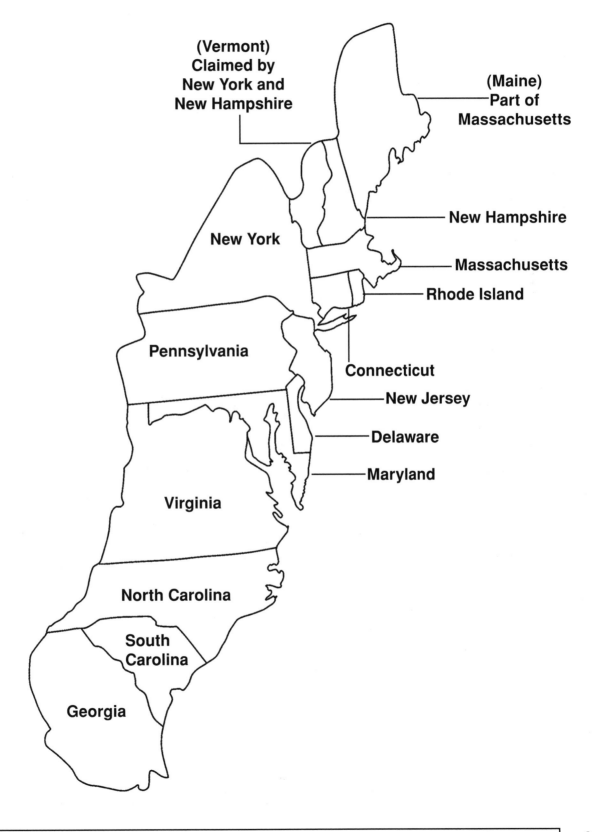

Give Me Liberty!

Patrick Henry's words made others want to fight for freedom.

The king of England ruled the thirteen American colonies. Some men were loyal to the king. They did not want to break away from his rule. They were called Loyalists. Some men wanted liberty. They wanted to be free to rule themselves. They were called Patriots.

A group of men met to talk about what should be done. Some spoke for peace. Others talked of war. A man named Patrick Henry stood up to speak. "Give me liberty, or give me death!" he said.

No one knows which side fired the first shot in the war. It happened near Boston on April 19, 1775. It became known as the "shot heard 'round the world."

The Patriots won the war. They created a new government. Their new country would have no king. In the new country, all men would have the right to liberty, the right to be free.

Nonfiction Reading Practice, Grade 3 • EMC 3314 • ©2003 by Evan-Moor Corp.

Name _____

Give Me Liberty!

Fill in the bubble to answer each question or complete each sentence.

1. The American colonies were once ruled by _____.
   - Ⓐ the king of England
   - Ⓑ the Patriots
   - Ⓒ Patrick Henry
   - Ⓓ the Loyalists

2. Patrick Henry said, "Give me liberty, or give me death!" because he _____.
   - Ⓐ wanted to be ruled by the king
   - Ⓑ wanted to be respected
   - Ⓒ was willing to die to be free
   - Ⓓ was willing to leave the country

3. The first shot in the war between the king and the colonists happened near _____.
   - Ⓐ Philadelphia, Pennsylvania
   - Ⓑ Boston, Massachusetts
   - Ⓒ Charleston, South Carolina
   - Ⓓ New York City, New York

4. Which side fired the first shot in the war?
   - Ⓐ the British
   - Ⓑ the American colonists
   - Ⓒ the French
   - Ⓓ no one knows

5. When the Patriots won the war, they decided to _____.
   - Ⓐ have a king
   - Ⓑ have Patrick Henry be their leader
   - Ⓒ give all men the right to be free
   - Ⓓ call the country the United States

Bonus: On the back of this page, write another way of saying, "Give me liberty, or give me death!"

A New Nation

In 1776, American colonists were ruled by the king of England. They were tired of being ruled by a king. They wanted a new kind of rule. They wanted to vote on things like laws and taxes. King George III would not let them. The colonists said that they would no longer obey the king. They fought for the right to rule themselves.

When the colonists won the war, the colonies became a new nation. It was called the United States of America. The new nation needed to decide how it would be ruled. People in all thirteen states chose men to speak for them. These men wrote a document. It showed how the new nation would be ruled. They called this document the Constitution.

They did not want one person to have too much power, like a king has. They split the power to rule into three branches. One branch would make the laws. One branch would enforce the laws. One branch would explain the laws and make sure they followed the Constitution.

To make the Constitution into law, each state had to vote in favor of it. Delaware was the first state to vote in favor. Rhode Island was the last. After all of the states voted, the United States had a new kind of government. The men who helped to create it became known as the Founding Fathers.

The U.S. Capital

LEGISLATIVE

The White House

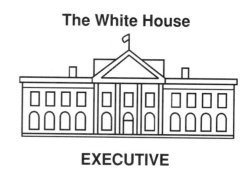

EXECUTIVE

The Supreme Court

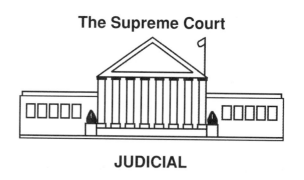

JUDICIAL

Name _____

A New Nation

Fill in the bubble to answer each question or complete each sentence.

1. In 1776, the American colonists were ruled by _____.
   Ⓐ the queen of England
   Ⓑ the king of England
   Ⓒ the Founding Fathers
   Ⓓ themselves

2. The document that showed how the new nation would be ruled was called _____.
   Ⓐ the Declaration of Independence
   Ⓑ the Constitution
   Ⓒ the Bill of Rights
   Ⓓ the Institution

3. Who were the Founding Fathers of the United States?
   Ⓐ men who fought in the war
   Ⓑ men who had a lot of children
   Ⓒ men who ruled England
   Ⓓ men who helped to create its new government

4. How did the Constitution become law?
   Ⓐ Each state voted for it.
   Ⓑ Each state voted against it.
   Ⓒ The Founding Fathers voted for it.
   Ⓓ Delaware voted for it.

5. Which of the following would the branches of the new government not do?
   Ⓐ enforce the laws
   Ⓑ make the laws
   Ⓒ break the laws
   Ⓓ explain the laws

Bonus: On the back of this page, write a "thank-you" note to the Founding Fathers.

An Independent Spirit

People in Europe said that the American colonists had an independent spirit. The colonists believed that people had rights. They thought that all men had the right to live, to be free, and to be happy. They also thought they had the right to vote on taxes and laws.

The colonists were ruled by King George III of England. He began to pass taxes and laws that they did not like. They did not have anyone to speak for them in England. They could not vote against these taxes. To protest the taxes, the colonists dumped tea in Boston Harbor. The king did not like their independent spirit. He passed more laws to try to control them. The colonists knew that they would have to fight to be free of the king's control.

All thirteen colonies joined together. On July 4, 1776, they declared their independence. Bells rang all day and into the night. People celebrated all over the new nation. King George III thought that the colonists would be afraid to fight his soldiers. They were not. They fought and won their freedom.

The Liberty Bell rang out in Philadelphia to declare American independence.

Nonfiction Reading Practice, Grade 3 • EMC 3314 • ©2003 by Evan-Moor Corp.

Name _____

An Independent Spirit

Fill in the bubble to answer each question.

1. Why did people in Europe say that the American colonists had an independent spirit?
   Ⓐ The colonists thought all men had the right to be leaders.
   Ⓑ The colonists thought all men had the right to be soldiers.
   Ⓒ The colonists thought all men had the right to be free.
   Ⓓ The colonists thought men should not have to follow any rules.

2. Why did the colonists want independence from King George III?
   Ⓐ They did not like the tea he sent to the colonies.
   Ⓑ He would not let them vote for or against laws and taxes.
   Ⓒ He said they were afraid to fight.
   Ⓓ He said they had to come back to England.

3. How many of the colonies joined in the fight against England?
   Ⓐ 12
   Ⓑ 20
   Ⓒ 13
   Ⓓ 14

4. Which word or phrase means about the same as **independent**?
   Ⓐ self-ruling
   Ⓑ dependent
   Ⓒ guided by others
   Ⓓ controlled

5. Which group of words describes the spirit of the American colonists?
   Ⓐ fearful, dependent, controlled
   Ⓑ shy, angry, hopeful
   Ⓒ nice, boring, smart
   Ⓓ brave, independent, free

Bonus: On the back of this page, explain why Americans have a celebration every July 4. Include three things Americans sometimes do on July 4 to celebrate.

Chief Seattle

Introducing the Topic

1. Reproduce page 23 for individual students, or make a transparency to use with a group or your whole class.

2. Present the illustration of the Puget Sound area, and read the caption and labels to connect the new vocabulary with a graphic representation.

Reading the Selection

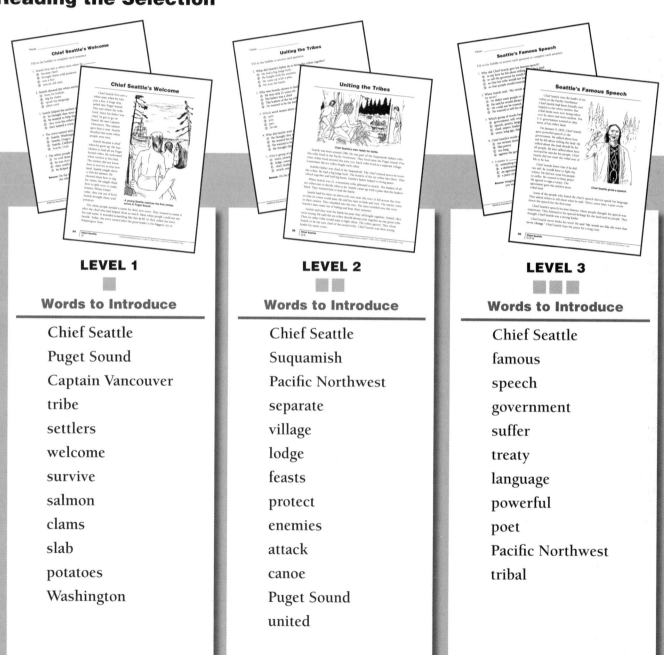

LEVEL 1
■

Words to Introduce

Chief Seattle

Puget Sound

Captain Vancouver

tribe

settlers

welcome

survive

salmon

clams

slab

potatoes

Washington

LEVEL 2
■ ■

Words to Introduce

Chief Seattle

Suquamish

Pacific Northwest

separate

village

lodge

feasts

protect

enemies

attack

canoe

Puget Sound

united

LEVEL 3
■ ■ ■

Words to Introduce

Chief Seattle

famous

speech

government

suffer

treaty

language

powerful

poet

Pacific Northwest

tribal

Map of the Puget Sound Area

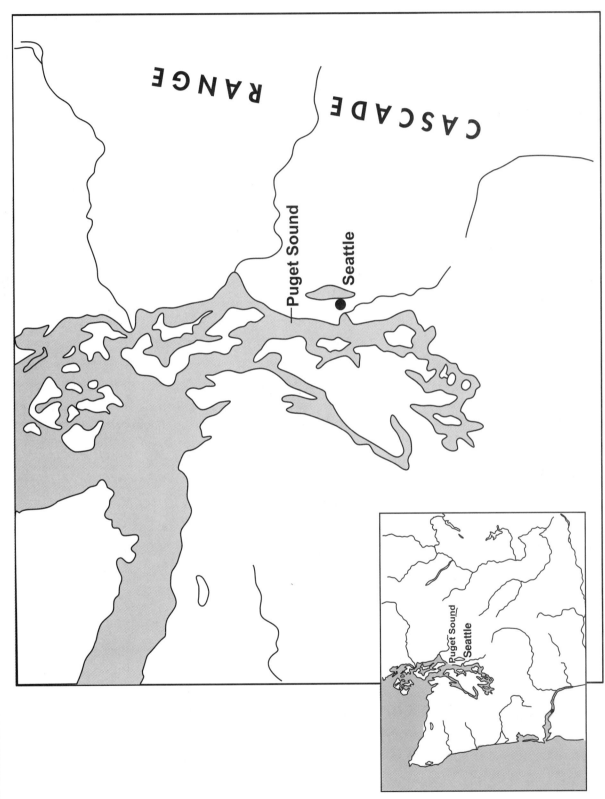

CASCADE RANGE

Puget Sound

Seattle

The Puget Sound area of what is now Washington State

Chief Seattle's Welcome

Chief Seattle first saw a white man when he was just a boy. A huge ship sailed into Puget Sound. This was where his tribe lived. Because his father was chief, he got to go on board. He met Captain Vancouver. The captain gave him a treat. Seattle decided that some white people were nice.

Seattle became a chief when he grew up. He was chosen to lead all six Puget Sound tribes. He welcomed white settlers to his land. The settlers did not know how to survive in this new land. Seattle taught them to fish for salmon. He showed them how to dig for clams. He taught them how to split trees to make houses. When winter came, they ran out of food. Seattle brought them wild potatoes.

A young Seattle watches the first whites arrive in Puget Sound.

The white people needed a name for their new town. They wanted to name it after the chief who had helped them so much. Most white people could not say his real name. It sounded something like **See-at-hl**. So they called the town Seattle. Today, the town named after the great leader is the biggest city in Washington State.

Name _____

Chief Seattle's Welcome

Fill in the bubble to complete each sentence.

1. Seattle first saw a white man when he _____.
   Ⓐ became chief
   Ⓑ brought them wild potatoes
   Ⓒ was a young boy
   Ⓓ was an old man

2. Seattle showed the white settlers how to _____.
   Ⓐ hunt for buffalo
   Ⓑ dig for clams
   Ⓒ speak his language
   Ⓓ plant corn

3. Seattle helped the settlers because _____.
   Ⓐ he thought they were mean
   Ⓑ he wanted to help them survive
   Ⓒ they took his tribe's land
   Ⓓ they named a town after him

4. The town named after the chief is _____.
   Ⓐ Seattle, Washington
   Ⓑ Seattle, Oregon
   Ⓒ Seattle, California
   Ⓓ Seattle, Utah

5. The white people named their town after Seattle because _____.
   Ⓐ he sold them the land
   Ⓑ he was their leader
   Ⓒ they could not say his real name
   Ⓓ he helped them so much

Bonus: On the back of this page, write why you think Chief Seattle welcomed the white settlers.

Uniting the Tribes

Chief Seattle's men ready for battle.

Seattle was born around 1786. He was part of the Suquamish Indian tribe. His tribe lived in the Pacific Northwest. They lived near the Puget Sound. Five other tribes lived around this area, too. Each tribe lived in a separate village. Sometimes the six tribes fought each other.

Seattle's father was chief of the Suquamish. The chief wanted peace between the tribes. He had a big lodge built. The leaders of the six tribes met there. They talked together and had big feasts. Seattle's father helped to bring peace.

When Seattle was 21, a mountain tribe planned to attack. The leaders of all six tribes met to decide what to do. Seattle came up with a plan that the leaders liked. They wanted him to lead the battle.

Seattle had his men cut down a fir tree near the river. It fell across the river so that no canoe could pass. He told his men to hide and wait. The enemy came in their canoes. They smashed into the tree. The men tumbled into the river. Seattle's men came out of hiding and beat their enemy.

Seattle said they won the battle because they all fought together. United, they were strong. He said the six tribes should always join together as one great tribe. Then no other tribe would want to fight them. The tribes agreed. They chose Seattle to be the new chief of the united tribe. Chief Seattle was their strong leader for many years.

Nonfiction Reading Practice, Grade 3 • EMC 3314 • ©2003 by Evan-Moor Corp.

Name _____

Uniting the Tribes

Fill in the bubble to answer each question.

1. What did Seattle's father do to bring the tribes together?
   - Ⓐ He had a big lodge built.
   - Ⓑ He fought with his enemies.
   - Ⓒ He came up with a plan.
   - Ⓓ He won the battle.

2. Why was Seattle chosen to lead the battle against the mountain tribe?
   - Ⓐ He was only 21 years old.
   - Ⓑ His father was a chief.
   - Ⓒ The leaders of the six tribes liked his plan.
   - Ⓓ He wanted to be the leader.

3. Which word means about the same as **unite**?
   - Ⓐ split
   - Ⓑ join
   - Ⓒ part
   - Ⓓ divide

4. Why did Seattle want to unite the tribes?
   - Ⓐ He thought they would be stronger joined together.
   - Ⓑ He wanted his tribe to keep helping the settlers.
   - Ⓒ He wanted to be the leader of all the tribes.
   - Ⓓ He thought they could build bigger villages together.

5. Which group of words has something to do with battle?
   - Ⓐ unity, joined, together
   - Ⓑ lodge, canoe, village
   - Ⓒ chief, leader, boss
   - Ⓓ attack, enemies, leader

Bonus: On the back of this page, write why Seattle was chosen as the new chief.

Seattle's Famous Speech

Chief Seattle was the leader of six tribes in the Pacific Northwest. Chief Seattle had been friendly and helpful to the white settlers. But tribal lands were now being taken over by more and more settlers. The U.S. government wanted to take more of his tribe's land.

On January 9, 1855, Chief Seattle gave a powerful speech to the government. He talked about how sad he felt about selling the land. He talked about how the land should be for all people. He also talked about how worried he was for his people. Chief Seattle did not want the tribal way of life to be lost.

Chief Seattle knew that if he did not sell, he would have to fight the whites. He did not want his people to suffer. He wanted to keep peace. He agreed to sign a treaty. The agreement gave the settlers more tribal land.

Chief Seattle gives a speech.

Some of the people who heard the chief's speech did not speak his language. They asked others to tell them what he said. Thirty years later, a poet wrote down the speech for the first time.

Chief Seattle's speech became famous. Many people thought his speech was important. They listened to his special feelings for the land and its people. They thought Chief Seattle was a strong leader.

Chief Seattle never broke his word. He said, **"My words are like the stars that never change."** Chief Seattle kept the peace for a long time.

Nonfiction Reading Practice, Grade 3 • EMC 3314 • ©2003 by Evan-Moor Corp.

Name _____

Seattle's Famous Speech

Fill in the bubble to answer each question or complete each sentence.

1. Why did Chief Seattle give his famous speech?
   - Ⓐ to say how he felt about selling his tribe's land
   - Ⓑ to tell the governor he would fight to keep the land
   - Ⓒ so that his tribe would not leave
   - Ⓓ so that people would remember him

2. When Seattle said, "My words are like the stars that never change," what did he mean?
   - Ⓐ He didn't want people to change.
   - Ⓑ He said he would always keep his word.
   - Ⓒ He could not be trusted.
   - Ⓓ He wanted to sell his tribe's land.

3. Which group of words has something to do with the tribe's land?
   - Ⓐ government, sell, treaty
   - Ⓑ speech, poetry, language
   - Ⓒ chief, expert, leader
   - Ⓓ years, long ago, thirty

4. Chief Seattle's words might have been changed because they were _____.
   - Ⓐ not written down for 30 years
   - Ⓑ like poetry
   - Ⓒ too long
   - Ⓓ against the government

5. A **treaty** is _____.
   - Ⓐ something sweet to eat
   - Ⓑ a declaration of war
   - Ⓒ an agreement between governments
   - Ⓓ a piece of paper

Bonus: Imagine that you are Chief Seattle. On the back of this page, write what you would say to the governor about selling your tribe's land.

The Boston Tea Party

Introducing the Topic

1. Reproduce page 31 for individual students, or make a transparency to use with a group or your whole class.

2. Present the map of Boston, and read the caption and labels to connect the new vocabulary with a graphic representation.

Reading the Selection

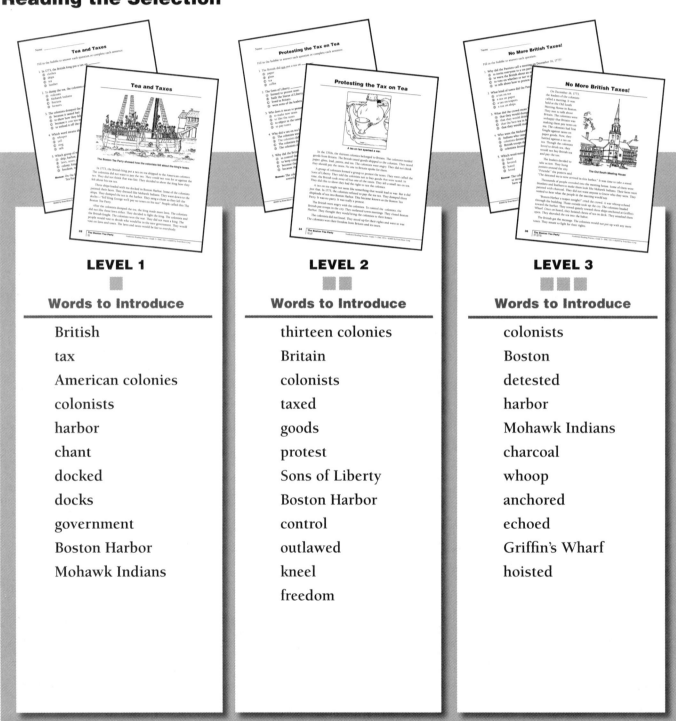

LEVEL 1	LEVEL 2	LEVEL 3
■	■ ■	■ ■ ■
Words to Introduce	**Words to Introduce**	**Words to Introduce**
British	thirteen colonies	colonists
tax	Britain	Boston
American colonies	colonists	detested
colonists	taxed	harbor
harbor	goods	Mohawk Indians
chant	protest	charcoal
docked	Sons of Liberty	whoop
docks	Boston Harbor	anchored
government	control	echoed
Boston Harbor	outlawed	Griffin's Wharf
Mohawk Indians	kneel	hoisted
	freedom	

Nonfiction Reading Practice, Grade 3 • EMC 3314 • ©2003 by Evan-Moor Corp.

Map of Boston Harbor

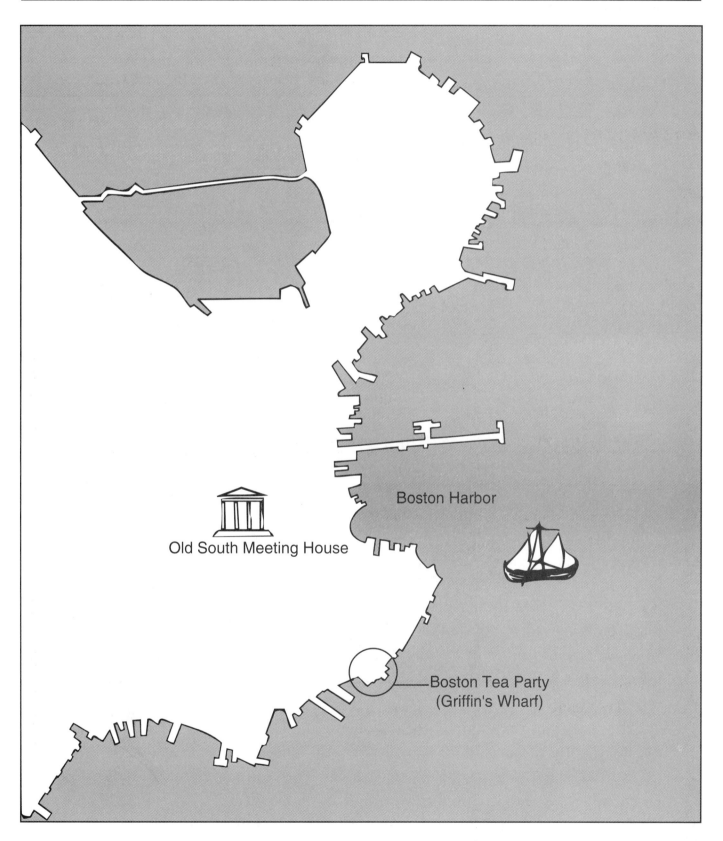

Old South Meeting House

Boston Harbor

Boston Tea Party
(Griffin's Wharf)

American colonists protested British tea taxes in Boston.

Tea and Taxes

The Boston Tea Party showed how the colonists felt about the king's taxes.

In 1773, the British king put a tax on tea shipped to the American colonies. The colonists did not want to pay the tax. They could not vote for or against the tax. They did not think that was fair. They decided to show the king how they felt about his tea tax.

Three ships loaded with tea docked in Boston Harbor. Some of the colonists painted their faces. They dressed like Mohawk Indians. They went down to the ships. They dumped the tea in the harbor. They sang a chant as they left the docks—"Tell King George we'll pay no taxes on his tea!" People called this the Boston Tea Party.

After the colonists dumped the tea, the king made more laws. The colonists did not like these laws either. They decided to fight the king. The colonists and the British fought. The colonists won the war. They did not want a king. The people would vote to decide who would be in the new government. They would vote on laws and taxes. The laws and taxes would be fair to everybody.

Name _____

Tea and Taxes

Fill in the bubble to answer each question or complete each sentence.

1. In 1773, the British king put a tax on _____.
   - Ⓐ clothes
   - Ⓑ ships
   - Ⓒ tea
   - Ⓓ lumber

2. To dump the tea, the colonists dressed like _____.
   - Ⓐ redcoats
   - Ⓑ Mohawk Indians
   - Ⓒ Patriots
   - Ⓓ farmers

3. The colonists dumped the tea _____.
   - Ⓐ because it tasted bad
   - Ⓑ to show how they felt about the tea tax
   - Ⓒ because it cost too much
   - Ⓓ to unload it off the ship quickly

4. Which word means about the same as **chant**?
   - Ⓐ whisper
   - Ⓑ yell
   - Ⓒ sing
   - Ⓓ talk

5. Which group of words has something to do with water?
   - Ⓐ ship, harbor, dock
   - Ⓑ laws, taxes, government
   - Ⓒ colony, king, war
   - Ⓓ freedom, unity, peace

Bonus: On the back of this page, write some things you know about the Boston Tea Party.

Protesting the Tax on Tea

A tea on tax sparked a war.

In the 1700s, the thirteen colonies belonged to Britain. The colonists needed goods from Britain. The British taxed goods shipped to the colonies. They taxed paper, glass, lead, paints, and tea. The colonists were angry. They did not think they should pay the taxes. No one in Britain spoke for them.

A group of colonists formed a group to protest the taxes. They were called the Sons of Liberty. They told the colonists not to buy goods that were taxed. In time, the British took away all but one of the taxes. They left a small tax on tea. They did this to show they had the right to tax the colonies.

A tax on tea might not seem like something that would lead to war. But it did just that. In 1773, the colonists refused to pay the tea tax. They dumped three shiploads of tea into Boston Harbor. This became known as the Boston Tea Party. It was no party. It was really a protest.

The British were angry with the colonists. To control the colonists, the British put troops in the city. They outlawed town meetings. They closed Boston Harbor. They thought they would bring the colonists to their knees.

The colonists did not kneel. They stood up for their rights and went to war. The colonists won their freedom from Britain and its taxes.

Name _____

Protesting the Tax on Tea

Fill in the bubble to answer each question or complete each sentence.

1. The British did <u>not</u> put a tax on _____.
   - Ⓐ paper
   - Ⓑ glass
   - Ⓒ tea
   - Ⓓ coffee

2. The Sons of Liberty _____.
   - Ⓐ formed to protest taxes
   - Ⓑ built the Statue of Liberty
   - Ⓒ lived in Britain
   - Ⓓ were sons of the leaders

3. What does it mean to **protest** the taxes?
   - Ⓐ to make new taxes
   - Ⓑ to like the taxes
   - Ⓒ to object to the taxes
   - Ⓓ to pay taxes

4. Why did a tax on tea lead to war?
   - Ⓐ The colonists were tired and hungry.
   - Ⓑ The colonists did not want to pay taxes to Britain.
   - Ⓒ The colonists did not like the ships in the harbor.
   - Ⓓ The colonists did not want to pay taxes to Boston.

5. Why did the British put troops in Boston?
   - Ⓐ to control the colonists
   - Ⓑ to keep colonists from drinking tea
   - Ⓒ because there was no room at the fort
   - Ⓓ because the troops needed a place to live

Bonus: The colonists protested taxes. On the back of this page, write about something that you would like to protest.

No More British Taxes!

On December 16, 1773, the leaders of the colonists called a meeting. It was held at the Old South Meeting House in Boston. They met to talk about Britain. The colonists were unhappy that Britain was making them pay taxes on tea. The colonists had first fought against taxes on paper goods. Now, they battled against a tax on tea. Although the colonists loved to drink tea, they would not buy British tea and pay the tax.

The Old South Meeting House

The leaders decided to take action. They hung posters around the city. "Friends!" the posters said. "The detested tea has now arrived in this harbor." It was time to take a stand.

Thousands of people crowded into the meeting house. Some of them wore blankets and feathers to make them look like Mohawk Indians. Their faces were painted with charcoal. They did not want anyone to know who they were. They waited to hear what the people in the meeting would say.

"Boston Harbor, a teapot tonight!" cried the crowd. A war whoop echoed through the building. Those outside took up the cry. The colonists headed toward the harbor. They rowed quietly toward three ships anchored at Griffin's Wharf. Once on board, they hoisted chests of tea on deck. They smashed them open. They shoveled the tea into the harbor.

The British got the message. The colonists would not put up with any more taxes. They meant to fight for their rights.

Name _____

No More British Taxes!

Fill in the bubble to answer each question.

1. Why did the Patriots call a meeting on December 16, 1773?
   - Ⓐ to invite everyone to a tea party
   - Ⓑ to warn the British about an attack
   - Ⓒ to vote on whether to pay taxes on paper
   - Ⓓ to talk about how to protest the tax on tea

2. What kind of taxes did the Patriots first protest?
   - Ⓐ a tax on tea
   - Ⓑ a tax on paper
   - Ⓒ a tax on teapots
   - Ⓓ a tax on ships

3. What did the crowd mean by "Boston Harbor, a teapot tonight"?
   - Ⓐ that they would dump tea into the harbor and make it like a teapot
   - Ⓑ that they would drink tea on ships in the harbor
   - Ⓒ that the best tea in Boston could be found at the harbor
   - Ⓓ that they would make noise like a teapot's whistle

4. Who were the Mohawks at Boston Harbor?
   - Ⓐ Indians who came to help the colonists
   - Ⓑ colonists dressed to look like Indians
   - Ⓒ British troops dressed to look like Indians
   - Ⓓ colonists dressed to look like British troops

5. Which word means about the same as **detested**?
   - Ⓐ liked
   - Ⓑ favored
   - Ⓒ hated
   - Ⓓ loved

Bonus: The colonists wanted to take a stand against the tea tax. They put up posters to invite people to a meeting. On the back of this page, write what you would have written on the poster.

Amazon Rainforest

Introducing the Topic

1. Reproduce page 39 for individual students, or make a transparency to use with a group or your whole class.

2. Present the diagram of the rainforest, and read the caption and labels to connect the new vocabulary with a graphic representation.

Reading the Selection

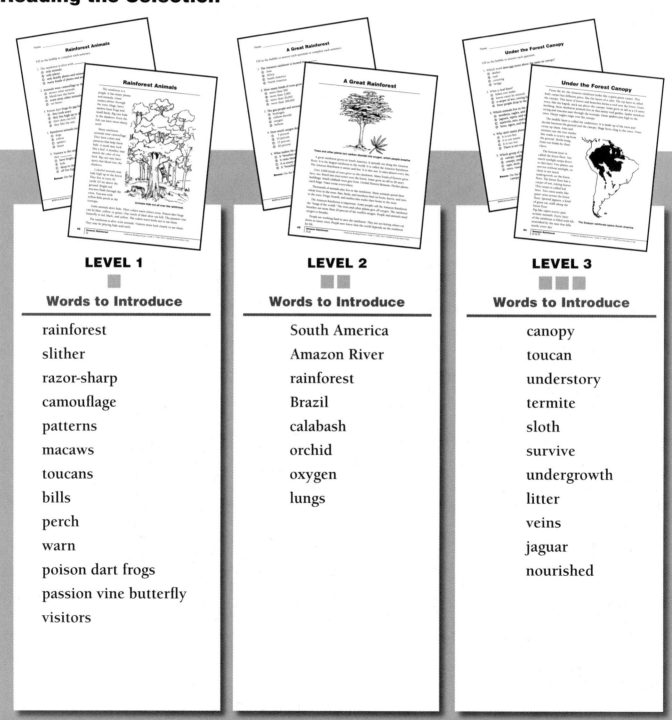

LEVEL 1

Words to Introduce

rainforest

slither

razor-sharp

camouflage

patterns

macaws

toucans

bills

perch

warn

poison dart frogs

passion vine butterfly

visitors

LEVEL 2

Words to Introduce

South America

Amazon River

rainforest

Brazil

calabash

orchid

oxygen

lungs

LEVEL 3

Words to Introduce

canopy

toucan

understory

termite

sloth

survive

undergrowth

litter

veins

jaguar

nourished

Nonfiction Reading Practice, Grade 3 • EMC 3314 • ©2003 by Evan-Moor Corp.

Amazon Rainforest

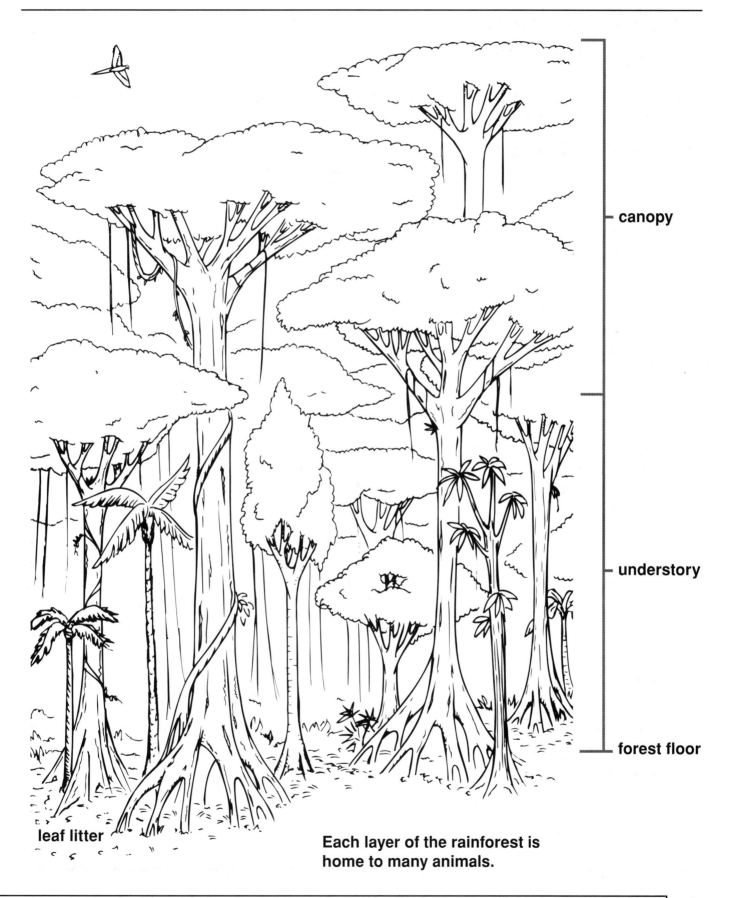

canopy

understory

forest floor

leaf litter

Each layer of the rainforest is home to many animals.

Rainforest Animals

The rainforest is a jungle. It has many plants and animals. Giant snakes slither through the trees. Huge, hairy spiders hunt frogs and small birds. Big cats hide in the shadows. Even the fish can have razor-sharp teeth.

Many rainforest animals wear camouflage. They have colors and patterns that help them hide. A moth may look like a leaf. A monkey may match the color of tree bark. Big cats may have spots that blend into the shadows.

Colorful animals may hide high up in the forest. They live in trees 30 yards (27 m) above the ground. Bright red macaws flash through the trees. Toucans with yellow bills perch in the treetops.

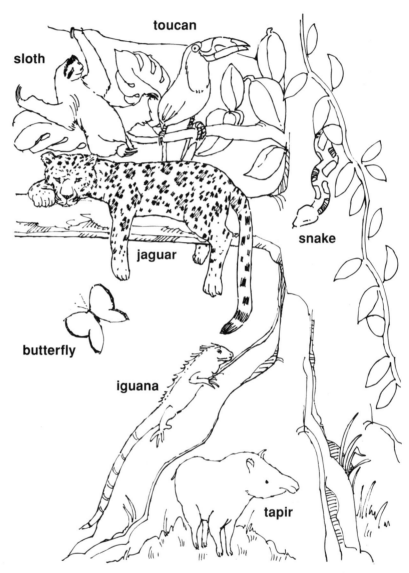

Animals hide out all over the rainforest.

Some animals don't hide. Their colors warn others away. Poison dart frogs can be blue, yellow, or green. One touch of their skin can kill. The passion vine butterfly is red, black, and yellow. The colors warn birds not to eat them.

The rainforest is alive with animals. Visitors must look closely to see them. They may be playing hide-and-seek.

Name _____

Rainforest Animals

Fill in the bubble to complete each sentence.

1. The rainforest is alive with _____.
   - Ⓐ only animals
   - Ⓑ only plants
   - Ⓒ only deadly plants and animals
   - Ⓓ many kinds of plants and animals

2. Animals wear camouflage so they can _____.
   - Ⓐ attract other animals
   - Ⓑ blend into the forest
   - Ⓒ scare away other animals
   - Ⓓ see better

3. Poison dart frogs do <u>not</u> hide, because _____.
   - Ⓐ they look scary
   - Ⓑ they live high up in the trees
   - Ⓒ their skin can kill
   - Ⓓ they like the sun

4. Rainforest animals include _____.
   - Ⓐ dogs
   - Ⓑ zebras
   - Ⓒ spiders
   - Ⓓ bears

5. Visitors to the rainforest must look closely to see most animals because they _____.
   - Ⓐ have bright colors
   - Ⓑ hide
   - Ⓒ sleep in the open
   - Ⓓ all live high in the trees

Bonus: On the back of this page, list the rainforest animals you know.

A Great Rainforest

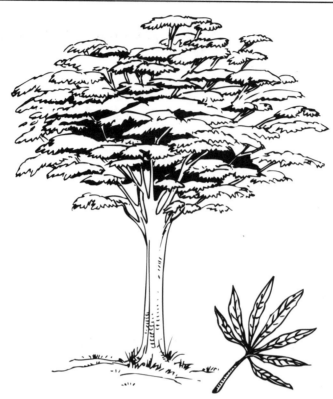

Trees and other plants turn carbon dioxide into oxygen, which people breathe.

A great rainforest grows in South America. It spreads out along the Amazon River. It is the largest rainforest in the world. It is called the Amazon Rainforest. The Amazon Rainforest is sunny and hot. It is also wet. It rains almost every day.

Over 3,000 kinds of trees grow in the rainforest. Many kinds of flowers grow here, too. Brazil nut trees tower over the forest. Some grow as tall as 20-story buildings. Small calabash trees make fruit. Orchid flowers blossom. Pitcher plants catch bugs. Vines twine everywhere.

Thousands of animals also live in the rainforest. Many animals spend their whole lives in the trees. Bats, birds, and monkeys feed on fruits, leaves, and nuts in the trees. Frogs, lizards, and snakes also make their home in the trees.

The Amazon Rainforest is important. Some people call the Amazon Rainforest the "lungs of the world." The trees and other plants give off oxygen. The rainforest breathes out more than 20 percent of the world's oxygen. People and animals need oxygen to breathe.

People are working hard to save the rainforest. They are not letting others cut down so many trees. People now know that the world depends on the rainforest for life.

Name _____

A Great Rainforest

Fill in the bubble to answer each question or complete each sentence.

1. The Amazon Rainforest is located in _____.
   - Ⓐ Asia
   - Ⓑ Africa
   - Ⓒ South America
   - Ⓓ North America

2. How many kinds of trees grow in the rainforest?
   - Ⓐ more than 300
   - Ⓑ more than 3,000
   - Ⓒ more than 30,000
   - Ⓓ more than 300,000

3. The gas people and animals need to breathe is called _____.
   - Ⓐ hydrogen
   - Ⓑ carbon dioxide
   - Ⓒ oxygen
   - Ⓓ helium

4. How much oxygen does the rainforest give the world?
   - Ⓐ 5 percent
   - Ⓑ 10 percent
   - Ⓒ 15 percent
   - Ⓓ 20 percent

5. What makes the rainforest the "lungs of the world"?
   - Ⓐ It "breathes out" more than 20 percent of the world's oxygen.
   - Ⓑ It rains there nearly every day.
   - Ⓒ It is sunny and hot.
   - Ⓓ It "breathes out" more than 20 percent of the world's carbon dioxide.

Bonus: On the back of this page, write why you think the rainforest should be saved.

Under the Forest Canopy

From the air, the Amazon Rainforest looks like a giant green carpet. This leafy carpet has different parts, like the layers of a cake. The top layer is called the canopy. This layer of leaves and branches forms a roof over the forest. Giant trees, like the kapok, stick out above the canopy. Some grow as tall as a 20-story building. Most rainforest animals live in this sunny roof garden. Spider monkeys swing and toucans soar through the treetops. Giant spiders nest high in the trees. Harpy eagles reign over the canopy.

The middle layer is called the understory. It is made up of the trees and shrubs between the ground and the canopy. Huge ferns cling to the trees. Vines twine up them. Ants and termites use the tree trunks like roads to scurry up from the ground. Sloths hang from tree limbs by their claws.

The bottom layer is called the forest floor. Not much sunlight seeps down to this layer. Few plants can survive without sunlight, so there is not much undergrowth on the forest floor. The forest floor has a carpet of wet, rotting leaves. This carpet is called leaf litter. Tree roots snake like giant veins across the forest floor. Spotted jaguars, a kind of giant cat, stalk along the forest floor. Pig-like tapirs scurry past termite mounds. Every layer of the rainforest is filled with life, nourished by the rain that falls nearly every day.

The Amazon Rainforest spans South America.

Nonfiction Reading Practice, Grade 3 • EMC 3314 • ©2003 by Evan-Moor Corp.

Name _____

Under the Forest Canopy

Fill in the bubble to answer each question.

1. Which word does <u>not</u> mean about the same as **canopy**?
   - Ⓐ shelter
   - Ⓑ roof
   - Ⓒ covering
   - Ⓓ bridge

2. What is **leaf litter**?
   - Ⓐ fallen tree limbs
   - Ⓑ leaves eaten by animals
   - Ⓒ a carpet of wet, rotting leaves
   - Ⓓ litter people drop in the rainforest

3. Which animals live in the rainforest canopy?
   - Ⓐ monkeys, eagles, and spiders
   - Ⓑ jaguars, tapirs, and termites
   - Ⓒ squirrels, ants, and sloths
   - Ⓓ lions, tigers, and bears

4. Why don't many plants grow on the forest floor?
   - Ⓐ It is too hot.
   - Ⓑ It is too sunny.
   - Ⓒ It is too wet.
   - Ⓓ There is not enough sunlight.

5. Which group of words describes the layers of the rainforest?
   - Ⓐ canopy, understory, leaf litter
   - Ⓑ canopy, understory, forest floor
   - Ⓒ tapir, sloth, squirrel
   - Ⓓ trees, vines, leaf litter

Bonus: On the back of this page, write a sentence that explains how the rainforest canopy is like a roof. Then tell what might be found beneath that roof.

Auroras

Introducing the Topic

1. Reproduce page 47 for individual students, or make a transparency to use with a group or your whole class.

2. Present the diagram of the aurora, and read the caption and labels to connect the new vocabulary with a graphic representation.

Reading the Selection

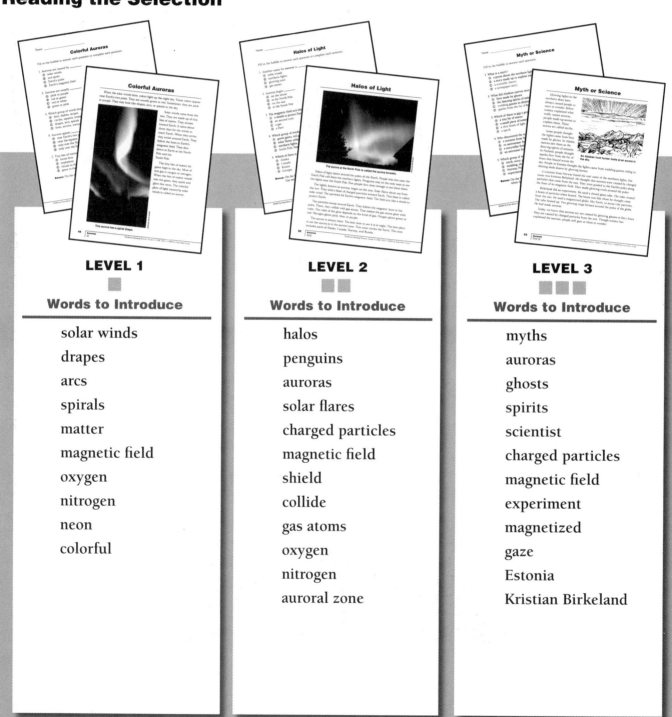

LEVEL 1

Words to Introduce

solar winds

drapes

arcs

spirals

matter

magnetic field

oxygen

nitrogen

neon

colorful

LEVEL 2

Words to Introduce

halos

penguins

auroras

solar flares

charged particles

magnetic field

shield

collide

gas atoms

oxygen

nitrogen

auroral zone

LEVEL 3

Words to Introduce

myths

auroras

ghosts

spirits

scientist

charged particles

magnetic field

experiment

magnetized

gaze

Estonia

Kristian Birkeland

An Aurora

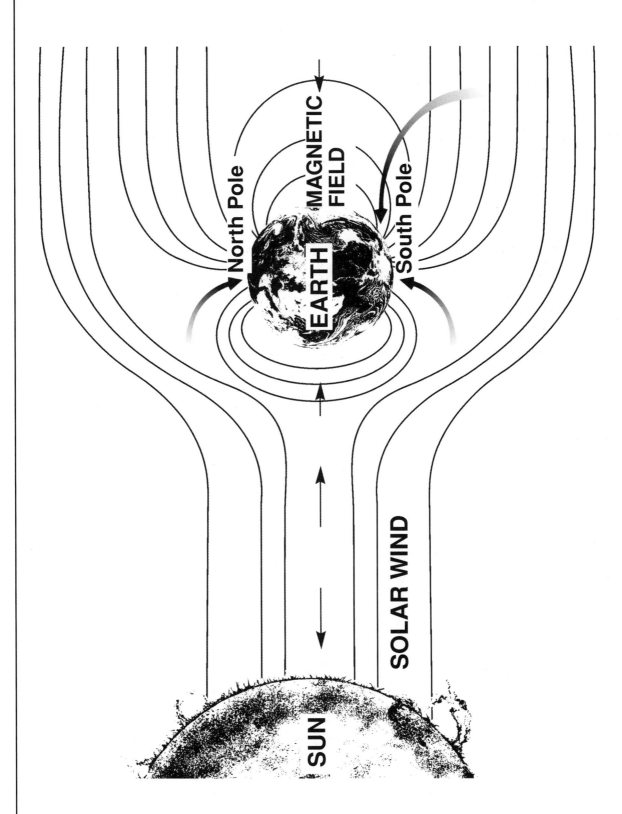

Auroras are formed when solar wind hits gases near Earth's poles.

Labels within the diagram: North Pole, MAGNETIC FIELD, South Pole, EARTH, SOLAR WIND, SUN

Colorful Auroras

When the solar winds blow, colors light up the night sky. These colors appear near Earth's two poles. They are usually green or red. Sometimes, they are pink or purple. They may look like drapes, arcs, or spirals in the sky.

photo by Jouni Jussila

This aurora has a spiral shape.

Solar winds come from the sun. They are made up of tiny bits of matter. They stream toward Earth. It takes about three days for the winds to reach Earth. When they arrive, they swish around Earth. They follow the lines in Earth's magnetic field. They dive down to Earth at the North Pole and the South Pole.

The tiny bits of matter hit gases high in the sky. Most of this gas is oxygen or nitrogen. When the bits of matter smash into the gases, they spark and glow like neon. The colorful glow of light caused by solar winds is called an aurora.

Name _____

Colorful Auroras

Fill in the bubble to answer each question or complete each sentence.

1. Auroras are caused by _____.
   - Ⓐ solar winds
   - Ⓑ sun spots
   - Ⓒ Earth's poles
   - Ⓓ Earth's magnetic field

2. Auroras are usually _____.
   - Ⓐ pink or purple
   - Ⓑ red or green
   - Ⓒ red or white
   - Ⓓ green or pink

3. Which group of words describes how auroras may look?
   - Ⓐ dots, dashes, stripes
   - Ⓑ circles, squares, triangles
   - Ⓒ drapes, arcs, spirals
   - Ⓓ lines, arrows, waves

4. Auroras appear _____.
   - Ⓐ near Earth's two poles
   - Ⓑ near the equator
   - Ⓒ only over the North Pole
   - Ⓓ only over the South Pole

5. Tiny bits of matter that come from the sun spark _____.
   - Ⓐ forest fires
   - Ⓑ explosions
   - Ⓒ clouds in the sky
   - Ⓓ gases in the sky

Bonus: On the back of this page, write what you know about auroras.

Halos of Light

The aurora at the North Pole is called the aurora borealis.

Halos of light dance around the poles of the Earth. People who live near the North Pole call them the northern lights. Penguins may be the only ones to see the lights near the South Pole. Few people live close enough to see them there.

The lights, known as auroras, begin on the sun. Solar flares shoot out from the sun. They send a blast of charged particles toward Earth. This blast is called solar wind. The particles hit Earth's magnetic field. The field acts like a shield to protect Earth.

The particles sweep around Earth. They follow the magnetic lines to the poles. There, they collide with gas atoms. That makes the gas atoms glow with color. The color of the glow depends on the kind of gas. Oxygen glows green or red. Nitrogen glows pink, blue, or purple.

The aurora is always there. The best time to see it is at night. The best place to see the aurora is in the auroral zone. This zone circles the Earth. The zone includes parts of Alaska, Canada, Norway, and Russia.

Nonfiction Reading Practice, Grade 3 • EMC 3314 • ©2003 by Evan-Moor Corp.

Name _____

Halos of Light

Fill in the bubble to answer each question or complete each sentence.

1. Another name for **auroras** is _____.
   - Ⓐ solar winds
   - Ⓑ northern lights
   - Ⓒ glowing stars
   - Ⓓ gas atoms

2. Auroras begin _____.
   - Ⓐ on the moon
   - Ⓑ at the North Pole
   - Ⓒ on the sun
   - Ⓓ at the South Pole

3. The magnetic field acts likes _____.
   - Ⓐ a shield to protect Earth
   - Ⓑ an auroral zone
   - Ⓒ a gas
   - Ⓓ a flare

4. Which group of words relate to the sun?
   - Ⓐ green gases, red gases, pink gases, purple gases
   - Ⓑ solar flares, solar wind, charged particles
   - Ⓒ northern lights, gas atoms, magnetic lines
   - Ⓓ South Pole, North Pole, auroral zone

5. Which of these is <u>not</u> one of the best places to see auroras?
   - Ⓐ Alaska
   - Ⓑ Canada
   - Ⓒ Russia
   - Ⓓ Georgia

Bonus: On the back of this page, write a poem about the northern lights. Use words from "Halos of Light."

Myth or Science?

An Alaskan Inuit hunter looks at an aurora in the sky.

Glowing lights in the northern skies have always caused people to stare in wonder. Before science explained what really causes auroras, people made up stories to explain them. These stories are called myths.

Some people thought the lights came from fires made by ghosts. In Alaska, natives saw them as the dancing spirits of animals. In Finland, people thought sparks flew from the fur of foxes that blazed across the sky. People in Estonia thought the lights came from wedding guests riding in shining sleds drawn by glowing horses.

A scientist from Norway found the real cause of the northern lights. His name was Kristian Birkeland. He thought that auroras were caused by charged particles that came from the sun. They were guided to the Earth's poles along the lines of its magnetic field. They made glowing ovals around the poles.

Birkeland did an experiment. He used a closed glass tube. The tube created a beam of particles when heated. The beam was like those he thought came from the sun. He used a magnetized globe, like Earth, to attract the particles. The tube heated up. Two glowing rings formed around the poles of the globe. He had made auroras.

Today, we know that auroras are not caused by glowing ghosts or fiery foxes. They are caused by charged particles from the sun. Though science has explained the auroras, people still gaze at them in wonder.

Nonfiction Reading Practice, Grade 3 • EMC 3314 • ©2003 by Evan-Moor Corp.

Name _____

Myth or Science?

Fill in the bubble to answer each question.

1. What is a myth?
   - Ⓐ a poem about the northern lights
   - Ⓑ a story made up to explain natural events
   - Ⓒ a scientific theory
   - Ⓓ a newspaper story

2. What did Alaskan natives once think caused the northern lights?
   - Ⓐ fires made by ghosts
   - Ⓑ the dancing spirits of animals
   - Ⓒ wedding guests in shining sleds
   - Ⓓ sparks from the fur of foxes

3. Which of these is <u>not</u> a good definition for the word **particle**?
   - Ⓐ a tiny bit of matter
   - Ⓑ a small piece of something solid
   - Ⓒ a thin beam of light
   - Ⓓ a speck

4. Who discovered the real cause of auroras?
   - Ⓐ a scientist from Norway
   - Ⓑ an astronomer from Finland
   - Ⓒ a storyteller from Alaska
   - Ⓓ an astronaut from Houston

5. Which group of words has something to with science?
   - Ⓐ myth, story, ghost
   - Ⓑ wedding, sleds, foxes
   - Ⓒ Norway, Finland, Alaska
   - Ⓓ experiment, glass tube, magnetized globe

Bonus: On the back of this page, write a sentence that explains what happened when the tube in Birkeland's experiment was heated.

Poison Dart Frogs

Introducing the Topic

1. Reproduce page 55 for individual students, or make a transparency to use with a group or your whole class.

2. Present the drawing of the life cycle of the poison dart frog, and read the caption and labels to connect the new vocabulary with a graphic representation.

Reading the Selection

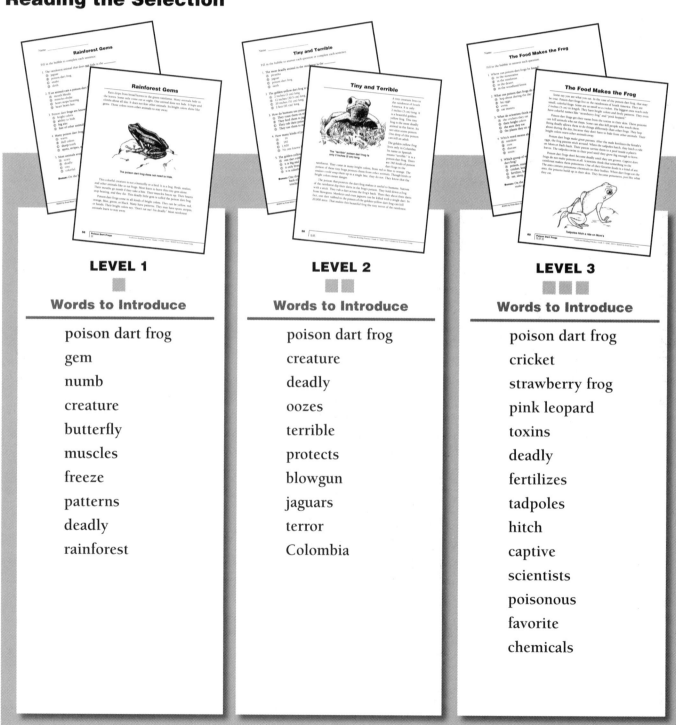

LEVEL 1
Words to Introduce

poison dart frog

gem

numb

creature

butterfly

muscles

freeze

patterns

deadly

rainforest

LEVEL 2
Words to Introduce

poison dart frog

creature

deadly

oozes

terrible

protects

blowgun

jaguars

terror

Colombia

LEVEL 3
Words to Introduce

poison dart frog

cricket

strawberry frog

pink leopard

toxins

deadly

fertilizes

tadpoles

hitch

captive

scientists

poisonous

favorite

chemicals

Nonfiction Reading Practice, Grade 3 • EMC 3314 • ©2003 by Evan-Moor Corp.

Poison Dart Frogs

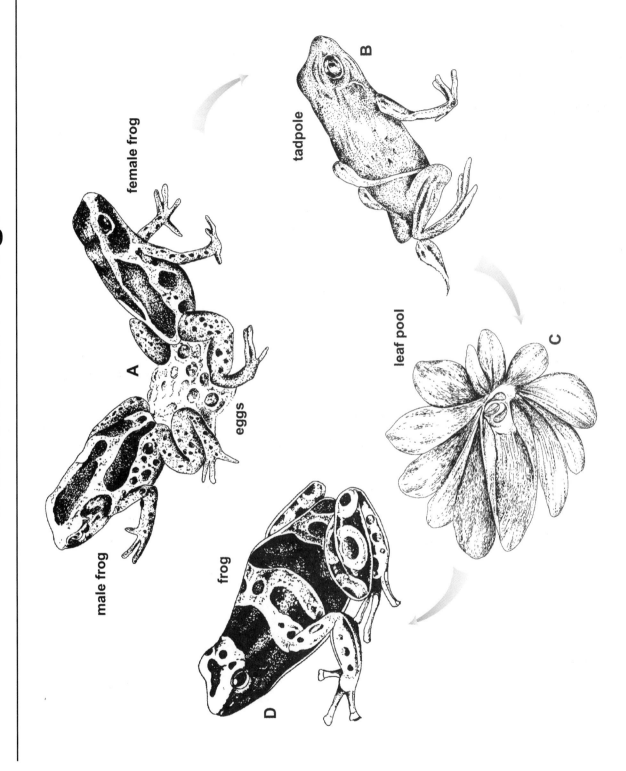

female frog

male frog

A

eggs

tadpole

B

leaf pool

C

frog

D

Poison dart frogs help their offspring survive.

Rainforest Gems

Rain drips from broad leaves in the green rainforest. Many animals hide in the leaves. Some only come out at night. One animal does not hide. It hops and climbs about all day. It does not fear other animals. Its bright colors shine like gems. Those colors warn other animals to stay away.

The poison dart frog does not need to hide.

This colorful creature is not a butterfly or a bird. It is a frog. Birds, snakes, and other animals like to eat frogs. Most learn to leave this tiny gem alone. Their mouths go numb if they take a bite. Their muscles freeze up. Their hearts stop beating, and they die. This deadly little gem is called the poison dart frog.

Poison dart frogs come in all kinds of bright colors. They can be yellow, red, orange, blue, green, or black. Many have patterns. They may have spots, stripes, or bands. Their bright colors say, "Don't eat me! I'm deadly." Most rainforest animals learn to stay away.

Name _____

Rainforest Gems

Fill in the bubble to complete each sentence.

1. The rainforest animal that does <u>not</u> hide is the _____.
   - Ⓐ jaguar
   - Ⓑ poison dart frog
   - Ⓒ snake
   - Ⓓ sloth

2. If an animal eats a poison dart frog, its _____.
   - Ⓐ mouth bleeds
   - Ⓑ muscles shake
   - Ⓒ heart stops beating
   - Ⓓ heart beats fast

3. Poison dart frogs are known for their _____.
   - Ⓐ bright colors
   - Ⓑ ability to hide
   - Ⓒ big size
   - Ⓓ fear of other animals

4. Many poison dart frogs have _____.
   - Ⓐ warts
   - Ⓑ dull colors
   - Ⓒ sharp teeth
   - Ⓓ spots, stripes, or bands

5. Most animals avoid poison dart frogs because they are _____.
   - Ⓐ scary
   - Ⓑ deadly
   - Ⓒ tiny
   - Ⓓ ugly

Bonus: On the back of this page, write four facts about poison dart frogs.

Tiny and Terrible

The "terrible" poison dart frog is only 2 inches (5 cm) long.

A tiny creature lives in the rainforest of South America. It is only 2 inches (5 cm) long. It is a beautiful golden-yellow frog. This tiny frog is the most deadly animal in the forest. Its wet skin oozes poison. One drop of this poison can kill an adult.

The golden-yellow frog lives only in Colombia. Its name in Spanish means "terrible." It is a poison dart frog. There are 140 kinds of poison dart frogs in the rainforest. They come in many bright colors, from red to blue to orange. The poison of these tiny frogs protects them from other animals. Although birds or snakes could snap them up in a single bite, they do not. They know that the bright colors mean danger.

The poison that protects the dart frog makes it useful to humans. Natives of the rainforest dip their darts in the frog's poison. They hold down a frog with a stick. They rub a dart across the frog's back. Then they shoot their darts from blowguns. Monkeys and even jaguars can be killed with a single dart. In fact, one dart rubbed in the poison of the golden-yellow dart frog can kill 20,000 mice. That makes this beautiful frog the tiny terror of the rainforest.

Nonfiction Reading Practice, Grade 3 • EMC 3314 • ©2003 by Evan-Moor Corp.

Name _____

Tiny and Terrible

Fill in the bubble to answer each question or complete each sentence.

1. The most deadly animal in the rainforest is the _____.
   - Ⓐ piranha
   - Ⓑ jaguar
   - Ⓒ poison dart frog
   - Ⓓ sloth

2. The golden-yellow dart frog is only _____.
   - Ⓐ 2 inches (5 cm) long
   - Ⓑ 12 inches (30.5 cm) long
   - Ⓒ 20 inches (51 cm) long
   - Ⓓ 2 feet (61 cm) long

3. How do humans use poison dart frogs?
   - Ⓐ They roast them on sticks and eat them.
   - Ⓑ They feed them to jaguars and monkeys.
   - Ⓒ They rub their poison on the darts they use to hunt.
   - Ⓓ They use them to make medicines.

4. How many kinds of poison dart frogs live in the rainforest?
   - Ⓐ 14
   - Ⓑ 140
   - Ⓒ 1,400
   - Ⓓ No one knows for sure.

5. The golden-yellow dart frog is called "terrible" because _____.
   - Ⓐ one dart rubbed on its back can kill 20,000 mice
   - Ⓑ it is big and scary looking
   - Ⓒ it only lives in Colombia
   - Ⓓ it is colorful

Bonus: One drop of the golden-yellow dart frog's poison can kill an adult. On the back of this page, write how you would capture a poison dart frog without touching it if you were a rainforest hunter.

The Food Makes the Frog

Some say you are what you eat. In the case of the poison dart frog, that may be true. Poison dart frogs live in the rainforests of South America. They are small, colorful frogs. Some are as small as a cricket. The biggest ones reach only 2 inches (5 cm) in length. They have bright colors and lively patterns. They even have colorful names like "strawberry frog" and "pink leopard."

Poison dart frogs get their name from the toxins in their skin. These poisons can kill animals who eat them. Some can also kill people who touch them. Being deadly allows them to do things differently than other frogs. They hop about during the day, because they don't have to hide from other animals. Their bright colors warn other animals away.

Poison dart frogs make great parents. After the male fertilizes the female's eggs, the frog parents stick around. When the tadpoles hatch, they hitch a ride on Mom or Dad's back. Their parent carries them to a pool inside a plant's leaves. The tadpoles swim in their pool until they grow big enough to leave.

Poison dart frogs don't become deadly until they are grown. Captive dart frogs do not make poisons at all. Scientists think that something in the rainforest makes them poisonous. One of their favorite foods is a kind of ant. The ants contain poisonous chemicals in their bodies. When dart frogs eat the ants, the poisons build up in their skin. They become poisonous, just like what they eat.

Tadpoles hitch a ride on Mom's back.

Nonfiction Reading Practice, Grade 3 • EMC 3314 • ©2003 by Evan-Moor Corp.

The Food Makes the Frog

Fill in the bubble to answer each question.

1. Where can poison dart frogs be found?
   - Ⓐ in the mountains
   - Ⓑ in the rainforest
   - Ⓒ in the desert
   - Ⓓ in the woodland forest

2. What can poison dart frogs do that many other frogs cannot?
   - Ⓐ hop about during the day
   - Ⓑ lay eggs
   - Ⓒ swim
   - Ⓓ eat insects

3. What do scientists think makes dart frogs poisonous?
   - Ⓐ the crickets they eat
   - Ⓑ their bright colors
   - Ⓒ the ants they eat
   - Ⓓ the plants they sit on

4. Which word means about the same as **poison**?
   - Ⓐ antidote
   - Ⓑ cure
   - Ⓒ disease
   - Ⓓ toxin

5. Which group of words has something to do with the life cycle of the poison dart frog?
   - Ⓐ poison, toxin, chemical
   - Ⓑ cricket, leopard, strawberry
   - Ⓒ fertilize, hatch, tadpole
   - Ⓓ eat, sleep, hunt

Bonus: On the back of this page, write a sentence that tells why poison dart frogs make great parents.

Pluto

Introducing the Topic

1. Reproduce page 63 for individual students, or make a transparency to use with a group or your whole class.

2. Present the diagram of the solar system, and read the caption and labels to connect the new vocabulary with a graphic representation.

Reading the Selection

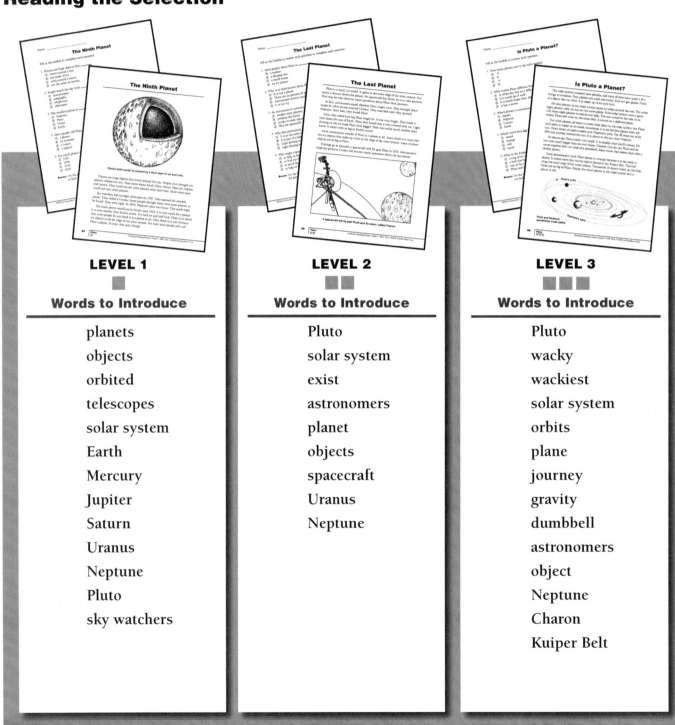

LEVEL 1
■

Words to Introduce

planets

objects

orbited

telescopes

solar system

Earth

Mercury

Jupiter

Saturn

Uranus

Neptune

Pluto

sky watchers

LEVEL 2
■ ■

Words to Introduce

Pluto

solar system

exist

astronomers

planet

objects

spacecraft

Uranus

Neptune

LEVEL 3
■ ■ ■

Words to Introduce

Pluto

wacky

wackiest

solar system

orbits

plane

journey

gravity

dumbbell

astronomers

object

Neptune

Charon

Kuiper Belt

Nonfiction Reading Practice, Grade 3 • EMC 3314 • ©2003 by Evan-Moor Corp.

The Solar System

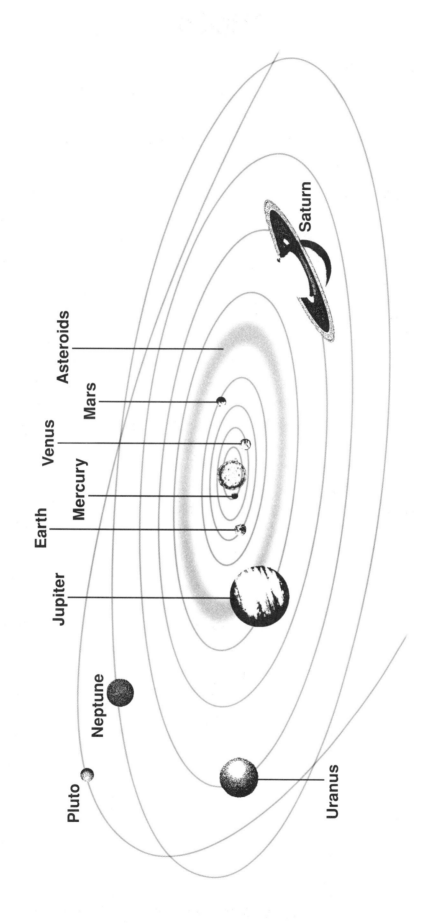

Pluto, the ninth planet in the solar system, may not be a planet after all!

The Ninth Planet

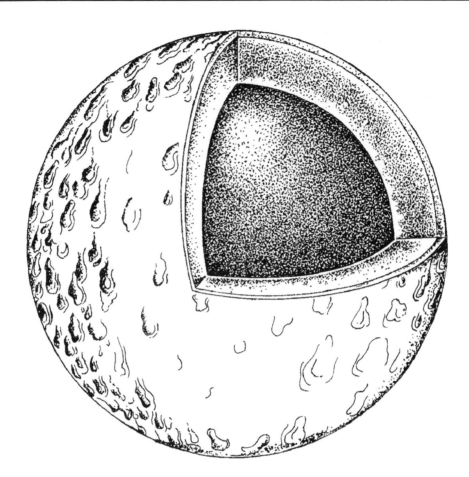

Pluto's solid center is covered by a thick layer of ice and rock.

Planets are large objects that travel around the sun. People once thought six planets orbited our sun. They knew about Earth, Mars, Venus, Mercury, Jupiter, and Saturn. They could not see other planets with their eyes. Early telescopes could not spot other planets.

Sky watchers had stronger telescopes by 1781. They spotted the seventh planet. They called it Uranus. Some people thought there were more planets to be found. They were right. In 1846, Neptune came into focus. That made eight.

The ninth planet would not be found until 1930. It is very small for a planet. It is even smaller than Earth's moon. It is half ice and half rock. Pluto is so small that some people do not think it is a planet at all. They think it is one of many icy objects at the far edge of our solar system. For now, most people still call Pluto a planet. In time, that may change.

Nonfiction Reading Practice, Grade 3 • EMC 3314 • ©2003 by Evan-Moor Corp.

The Ninth Planet

Fill in the bubble to complete each sentence.

1. Planets are large objects that _____.
   - Ⓐ travel around a sun
   - Ⓑ are made of ice
   - Ⓒ orbit around a moon
   - Ⓓ are the same as moons

2. People watch the sky with _____.
   - Ⓐ microscopes
   - Ⓑ telegraphs
   - Ⓒ telephones
   - Ⓓ telescopes

3. The smallest planet is _____.
   - Ⓐ Neptune
   - Ⓑ Pluto
   - Ⓒ Venus
   - Ⓓ Earth

4. Most people call Pluto _____.
   - Ⓐ a planet
   - Ⓑ an asteroid
   - Ⓒ a comet
   - Ⓓ a meteor

5. The ninth planet was found in _____.
   - Ⓐ 1781
   - Ⓑ 1846
   - Ⓒ 1930
   - Ⓓ 1830

Bonus: On the back of this page, write why you think it took sky watchers so long to find Pluto.

The Last Planet

Pluto is a small, icy world. It spins at the outer edge of the solar system. Not much is known about this planet. No spacecraft has flown by it to take pictures. That may be why there are more questions about Pluto than answers.

At first, astronomers asked whether Pluto might exist. They thought there might be other planets beyond Uranus. They searched until they spotted Neptune. Years later, they found Pluto.

Next, they asked how big Pluto might be. It was very bright. That made it look about the size of Earth. Then they found that it was covered with ice. Light shining on the ice made Pluto look bigger. Pluto was really much smaller than Earth. It wasn't even as big as Earth's moon.

Now, astronomers wonder if Pluto is a planet at all. Some think it is more like the icy objects that make up a belt at the edge of the solar system. Some of these objects are as big as Pluto.

If things go as planned, a spacecraft will fly past Pluto in 2016. Astronomers hope the pictures it takes will answer many questions about the last planet.

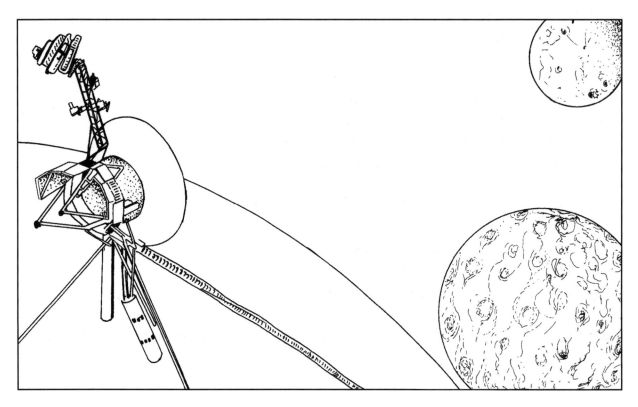

A spacecraft will fly past Pluto and its moon, called Charon.

Nonfiction Reading Practice, Grade 3 • EMC 3314 • ©2003 by Evan-Moor Corp.

Name _____

The Last Planet

Fill in the bubble to answer each question or complete each sentence.

1. Most people think Pluto is _____.
   - Ⓐ a meteor
   - Ⓑ a shining star
   - Ⓒ a small moon
   - Ⓓ an icy planet

2. Why is so little known about Pluto?
   - Ⓐ It is not a planet.
   - Ⓑ There are no pictures of it.
   - Ⓒ Astronomers haven't studied it.
   - Ⓓ It is too icy.

3. An **astronomer** is someone who _____.
   - Ⓐ studies stars, planets, comets, and galaxies
   - Ⓑ predicts the future
   - Ⓒ works in outer space
   - Ⓓ flies the spacecraft

4. Why did astronomers once think Pluto was as big as Earth?
   - Ⓐ It is at the outer edge of the solar system.
   - Ⓑ It is part of a belt of icy objects.
   - Ⓒ Light shining on its icy surface made it look bigger.
   - Ⓓ Light shining on its icy surface made it look smaller.

5. Why might a spacecraft fly past Pluto in 2016?
   - Ⓐ to help us learn more about the last planet
   - Ⓑ to find out if anyone lives there
   - Ⓒ to see if there are other planets beyond Pluto
   - Ⓓ to help us learn more about Neptune

Bonus: On the back of this page, write what you think astronomers will learn from the pictures that might be taken in 2016.

Is Pluto a Planet?

The solar system contains nine planets, and most of them have quite a few things in common. Four planets are solid and rocky. Four are gas giants. Pluto is a planet like no other. It is made up of ice and rock.

All nine planets in our solar system move in orbits around the sun. The other eight planets orbit the sun on the same plane. If the solar system were a giant CD, these eight planets would be one disk. The sun would be the hole at its center. Pluto isn't even on the same disk. It moves on a different plane.

The other planets all seem to know their place in the solar system, but Pluto can't seem to make up its mind. Sometimes it is the farthest planet from the sun. Other times, its path crosses over Neptune's orbit. For 20 years out of its 248-year journey around the sun, it is closer to the sun than Neptune.

As planets go, Pluto seems very small. It is smaller than Earth's moon. It's not even much bigger than its own moon, Charon. Gravity ties Pluto and its moon together like two ends of a dumbbell. Some think that makes them like a double planet.

Some astronomers think Pluto seems so strange because it is not really a planet. It seems more like the icy objects found in the Kuiper Belt. This belt rings the outer edge of the solar system. Thousands of objects make up this belt. Some are as big as Pluto. Maybe the ninth planet in the solar system isn't a planet at all!

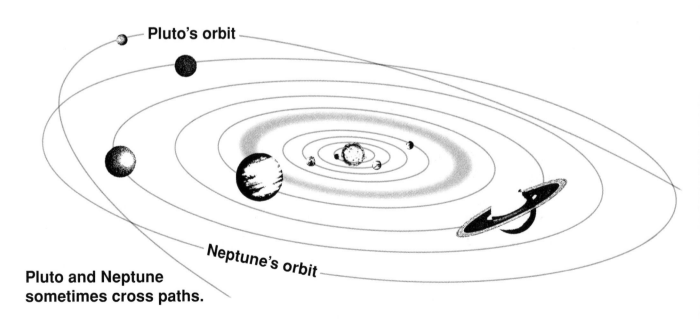

Pluto's orbit

Neptune's orbit

Pluto and Neptune sometimes cross paths.

Nonfiction Reading Practice, Grade 3 • EMC 3314 • ©2003 by Evan-Moor Corp.

Name _____

Is Pluto a Planet?

Fill in the bubble to answer each question.

1. How many planets are in the solar system?
   Ⓐ 8
   Ⓑ 10
   Ⓒ 9
   Ⓓ 20

2. What makes Pluto different from the other planets?
   Ⓐ It orbits the sun on a different plane.
   Ⓑ It is made up of rock.
   Ⓒ It is much larger than the other planets.
   Ⓓ It has a moon.

3. Which planet is sometimes farther from the sun than Pluto?
   Ⓐ Jupiter
   Ⓑ Neptune
   Ⓒ Uranus
   Ⓓ Earth

4. Which word does not mean about the same as **wacky**?
   Ⓐ weird
   Ⓑ strange
   Ⓒ odd
   Ⓓ usual

5. What is the Kuiper Belt?
   Ⓐ a ring of icy objects at the edge of the solar system
   Ⓑ a belt that holds the solar system together
   Ⓒ one of the rings around Saturn
   Ⓓ Pluto and its moon, Charon

Bonus: On the back of this page, write why you think Pluto is a planet, or why you believe it is not.

Robot Helpers

Introducing the Topic

1. Reproduce page 71 for individual students, or make a transparency to use with a group or your whole class.

2. Present the diagram of the robot, and read the caption and labels to connect the new vocabulary with a graphic representation.

Reading the Selection

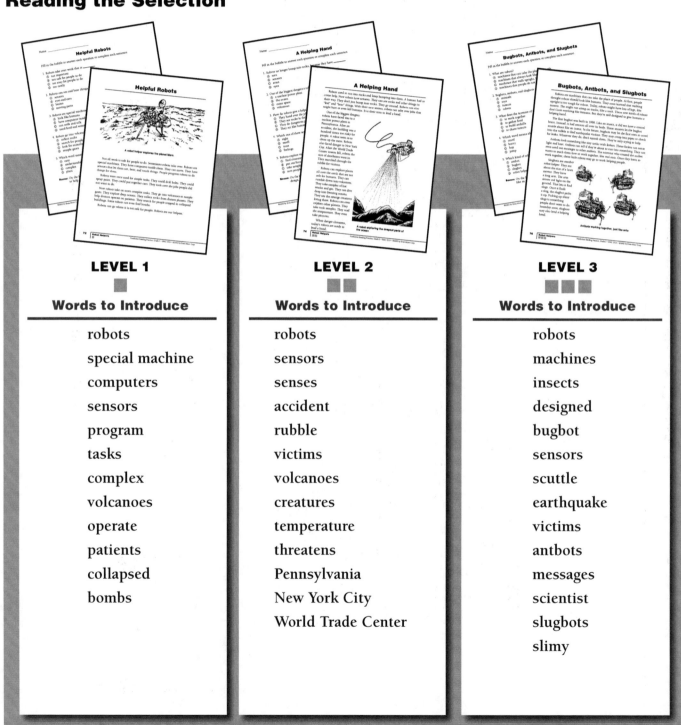

LEVEL 1
■

Words to Introduce

robots

special machine

computers

sensors

program

tasks

complex

volcanoes

operate

patients

collapsed

bombs

LEVEL 2
■ ■

Words to Introduce

robots

sensors

senses

accident

rubble

victims

volcanoes

creatures

temperature

threatens

Pennsylvania

New York City

World Trade Center

LEVEL 3
■ ■ ■

Words to Introduce

robots

machines

insects

designed

bugbot

sensors

scuttle

earthquake

victims

antbots

messages

scientist

slugbots

slimy

Nonfiction Reading Practice, Grade 3 • EMC 3314 • ©2003 by Evan-Moor Corp.

Surgical Robot Helper

Robot Control Computer (RCC)

color monitor

force sensor

cutting tool

bone motion monitor (BMM)

robot base

Robots help doctors heal patients.

Helpful Robots

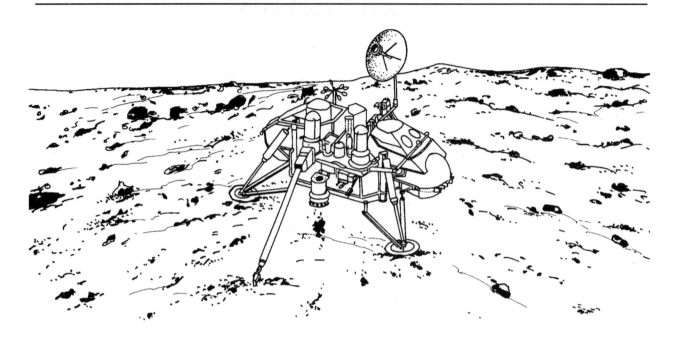

A robot helper explores the planet Mars.

Not all work is safe for people to do. Sometimes robots take over. Robots are special machines. They have computers inside them. They can move. They have sensors that let them see, hear, and touch things. People program robots to do things for them.

Robots were once used for simple tasks. They could drill holes. They could spray paint. They could put together cars. They took over the jobs people did not want to do.

Now robots take on more complex tasks. They go into volcanoes to sample gases. They explore deep oceans. They collect rocks from distant planets. They help doctors operate on patients. They search for people trapped in collapsed buildings. Some robots can even find bombs.

Robots can go where it is not safe for people. Robots are our helpers.

Nonfiction Reading Practice, Grade 3 • EMC 3314 • ©2003 by Evan-Moor Corp.

Name _____

Helpful Robots

Fill in the bubble to answer each question or complete each sentence.

1. Robots take over work that is _____.
   Ⓐ not important
   Ⓑ not safe for people to do
   Ⓒ too easy for people to do
   Ⓓ too costly

2. Robots can see and hear things because they have _____.
   Ⓐ sensors
   Ⓑ eyes and ears
   Ⓒ brains
   Ⓓ moving parts

3. Robots are special machines that _____.
   Ⓐ look like humans
   Ⓑ have computers inside them
   Ⓒ feel love
   Ⓓ need food and water

4. Robots go into volcanoes to _____.
   Ⓐ collect rocks
   Ⓑ search for people
   Ⓒ look for animals
   Ⓓ sample gases

5. Which word means the opposite of **simple**?
   Ⓐ easy
   Ⓑ understandable
   Ⓒ complex
   Ⓓ plain

Bonus: On the back of this page, write about something you would like a robot
to help you do.

A Helping Hand

Robots used to run into rocks and keep bumping into them. A human had to come help. Now robots have sensors. They can see rocks and other things in their way. They don't just bump into rocks. They go around them. Robots can also "feel" and "hear" things. With their new senses, robots can take over jobs that might hurt or even kill humans. It is their turn to lend a hand.

One of the biggest dangers robots have faced was in a nuclear power plant in Pennsylvania. After an accident, the building was a hundred times too risky for people. A robot went in to clean up the mess. Robots also faced danger in New York City. After the World Trade Center towers fell, robots the size of shoeboxes went in. They searched through the rubble for victims.

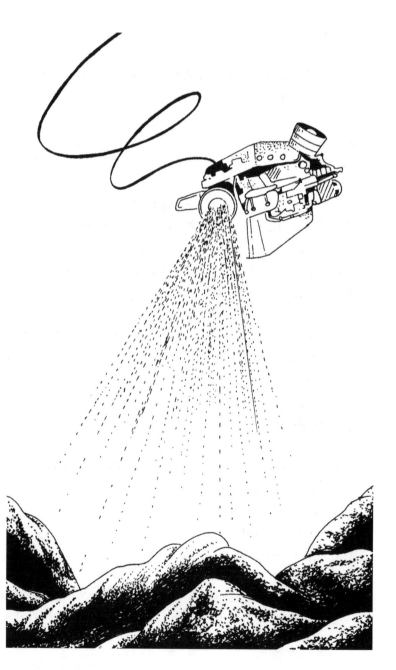

A robot is exploring the deepest parts of the ocean.

Robots can explore places all over the earth that are not safe for humans. They can rumble down into volcanoes. They take samples of hot smoke and gas. They can dive deep into freezing oceans. They see the strange creatures living there. Robots can even explore other planets. They take rock samples. They read the temperature. They even take pictures.

When danger threatens, today's robots are ready to lend a hand.

Name _____

A Helping Hand

Fill in the bubble to answer each question or complete each sentence.

1. Robots no longer bump into rocks, because they have _____.
   - Ⓐ ears
   - Ⓑ sensors
   - Ⓒ arms
   - Ⓓ eyes

2. One of the biggest dangers a robot has faced was in _____.
   - Ⓐ a nuclear power plant
   - Ⓑ the ocean
   - Ⓒ outer space
   - Ⓓ volcanoes

3. How do robots give a helping hand?
   - Ⓐ They hand over the jobs to humans.
   - Ⓑ They see rocks in their way.
   - Ⓒ They do dangerous jobs for humans.
   - Ⓓ They act like humans.

4. Which one of these senses do some robots have?
   - Ⓐ sight
   - Ⓑ smell
   - Ⓒ taste
   - Ⓓ feelings

5. Robots explore volcanoes, oceans, and other planets to _____.
   - Ⓐ find creatures
   - Ⓑ put out fires
   - Ⓒ take samples
   - Ⓓ save people

Bonus: On the back of this page, draw a picture of a robot helper of your own design. Write a sentence that tells what it can do.

Bugbots, Antbots, and Slugbots

Robots are machines that can take the place of people. At first, people thought robots should look like humans. They soon learned that walking upright is too tough for robots. Today, robots might have lots of legs, like insects. They might run along on tracks, like a tank. These new kinds of robots don't look anything like humans. But they're still designed to give humans a helping hand.

The first bugbot was built in 1988. Like an insect, it did not have a central brain. Instead, it had sensors all over its body. These sensors let the bugbot scuttle about like an insect. In the future, bugbots may be the first ones to crawl into the rubble to find earthquake victims. They may creep into pipes to check for leaks. Whatever they do, don't squash them. They're only trying to help.

Antbots look something like tiny tanks with feelers. These feelers can sense light and heat. Antbots can tell if they're about to run into something. They can even send out messages to other antbots. The scientist who created the antbot wants to teach them how to work together, like real ants. Once they learn to work together, these little robots may go to work helping people.

Slugbots are another robot helper. They are about the size of a lawn mower. They have a long arm. The arm shines red light on the ground. That lets it find slugs. Once it finds a slug, the slugbot picks it up. Picking up slimy slugs is something people don't want to do. Someday soon, slugbots may also lend a helping hand.

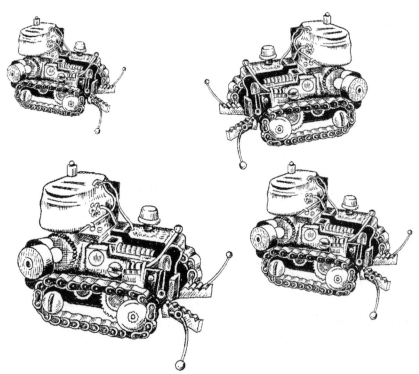

Antbots may someday work together, just like ants.

Name _____

Bugbots, Antbots, and Slugbots

Fill in the bubble to answer each question or complete each sentence.

1. What are robots?
   - Ⓐ machines that can take the place of people
   - Ⓑ machines that always look like humans
   - Ⓒ machines that walk upright, like people
   - Ⓓ machines that people do not like

2. Bugbots, antbots, and slugbots are _____.
   - Ⓐ animals
   - Ⓑ toys
   - Ⓒ insects
   - Ⓓ robots

3. What does the inventor of the antbot want to teach them to do?
   - Ⓐ to work together
   - Ⓑ to gather food
   - Ⓒ to build anthills
   - Ⓓ to chase insects

4. Which word means about the same as **scuttle**?
   - Ⓐ carry
   - Ⓑ hurry
   - Ⓒ hop
   - Ⓓ jump

5. Which kind of robot picks up slimy creatures?
   - Ⓐ antbot
   - Ⓑ bugbot
   - Ⓒ slugbot
   - Ⓓ robot helpers

Bonus: On the back of this page, write a sentence that explains how an antbot is like an ant.

Jane Goodall

Introducing the Topic

1. Reproduce page 79 for individual students, or make a transparency to use with a group or your whole class.

2. Present the map of Africa, and read the caption and labels to connect the new vocabulary with a graphic representation.

Reading the Selection

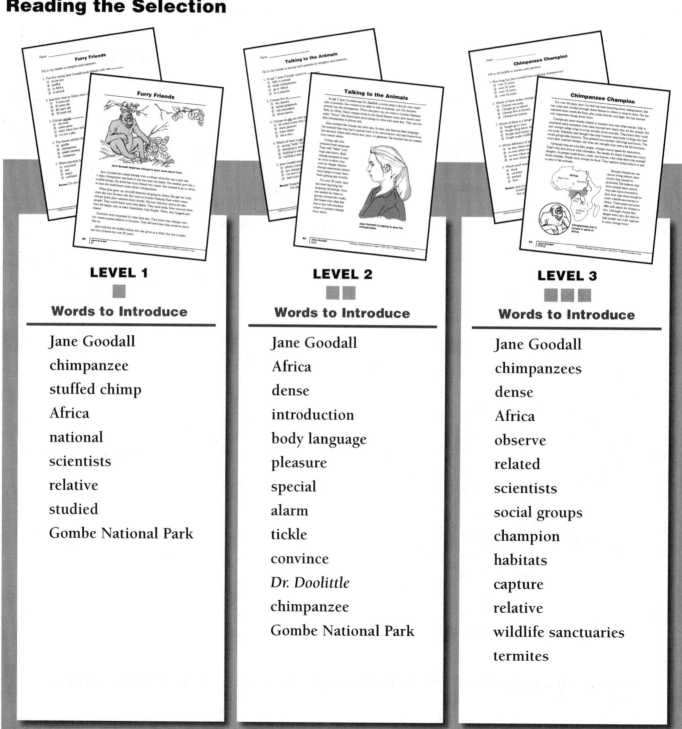

LEVEL 1
■

Words to Introduce

Jane Goodall

chimpanzee

stuffed chimp

Africa

national

scientists

relative

studied

Gombe National Park

LEVEL 2
■ ■

Words to Introduce

Jane Goodall

Africa

dense

introduction

body language

pleasure

special

alarm

tickle

convince

Dr. Doolittle

chimpanzee

Gombe National Park

LEVEL 3
■ ■ ■

Words to Introduce

Jane Goodall

chimpanzees

dense

Africa

observe

related

scientists

social groups

champion

habitats

capture

relative

wildlife sanctuaries

termites

Nonfiction Reading Practice, Grade 3 • EMC 3314 • ©2003 by Evan-Moor Corp.

Gombe Stream Game Preserve

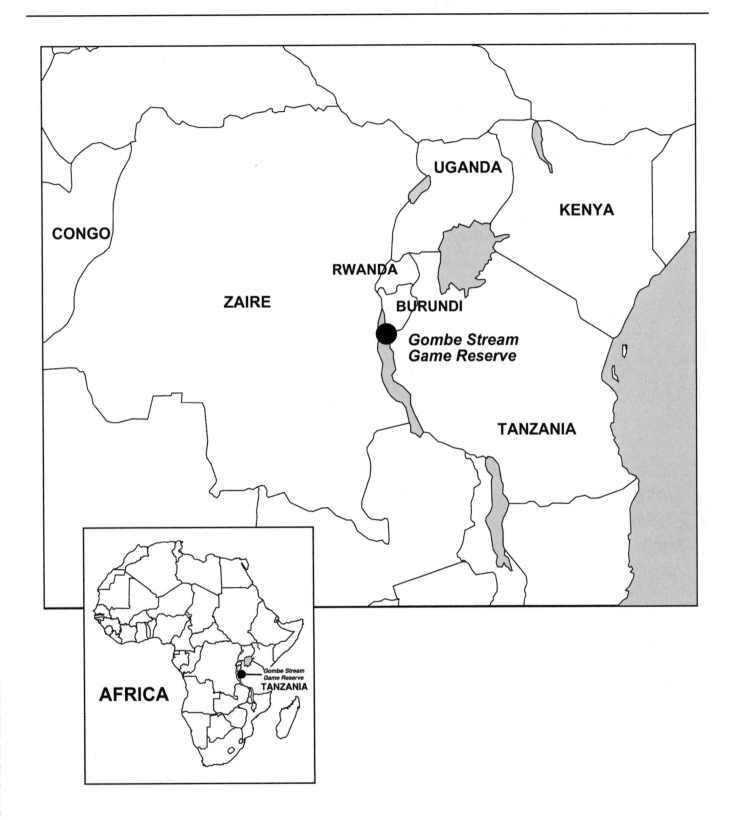

Jane Goodall began to study chimpanzees at the Gombe Stream Game Reserve.

Furry Friends

Jane Goodall observes chimps to learn more about them.

Jane Goodall first made friends with a chimp when she was a year old. A baby chimpanzee was born in the zoo near her home. Her mother gave her a stuffed chimp. She loved her furry friend very much. She wanted to go to Africa so that she could learn more about chimpanzees.

When Jane grew up, she still dreamed of going to Africa. She got her wish when she was 26 years old. She went to Gombe National Park where many chimps lived. Jane watched them closely. She saw that they were a lot like people. They could think and make plans. They used tools. They showed when they felt happy, sad, or mad. Sometimes, they fought. Often, they hugged and kissed.

Scientists were surprised by what Jane saw. They knew that chimps were the closest animal relative to humans. They did not know they acted so much like us.

Jane still has the stuffed chimp she was given as a child. She has studied her furry friends for over 30 years.

Name _____

Furry Friends

Fill in the bubble to complete each sentence.

1. The first chimp Jane Goodall made friends with was _____.
   - Ⓐ in the zoo
   - Ⓑ stuffed
   - Ⓒ in Africa
   - Ⓓ in school

2. Jane first went to Africa when she was _____.
   - Ⓐ 6 years old
   - Ⓑ 16 years old
   - Ⓒ 26 years old
   - Ⓓ 36 years old

3. Chimps <u>cannot</u> _____.
   - Ⓐ use tools
   - Ⓑ make plans
   - Ⓒ show when they feel happy
   - Ⓓ act out a play

4. The closest animal relation to humans is the _____.
   - Ⓐ gorilla
   - Ⓑ chimpanzee
   - Ⓒ spider monkey
   - Ⓓ orangutan

5. When scientists heard that chimps could use tools, they were _____.
   - Ⓐ surprised
   - Ⓑ sad
   - Ⓒ angry
   - Ⓓ confused

Bonus: On the back of this page, write four facts about chimpanzees.

Talking to the Animals

At age 7, Jane Goodall read *Dr. Doolittle,* a book about a doctor who could talk to animals. She wanted to be able to talk to animals, too. Her favorite animal was the chimpanzee. When she grew up, she went to Gombe National Park, in Africa. Many chimps lived in the dense forests there. Jane heard their noisy "hoots." She heard them drumming on trees with their feet. This was her first introduction to chimp talk.

Jane watched the chimps day after day. In time, she learned their language. She learned that they had a special bark to let others know they had found food. She learned which calls meant fear, pain, or pleasure. She learned that an uneasy hoot meant alarm.

Chimp talk also included body language. They said "hello" with hugs and kisses. Male chimps stomped or beat on trees to show they were in charge. Mother chimps sometimes tickled their babies to keep them from getting into trouble.

For over 30 years, Jane has been learning the language of chimps. Now, she speaks for them to groups around the world. She hopes that what she has to say will convince others to protect chimps from harm.

Jane Goodall is helping to save the chimpanzees.

Nonfiction Reading Practice, Grade 3 • EMC 3314 • ©2003 by Evan-Moor Corp.

Name _____

Talking to the Animals

Fill in the bubble to answer each question or complete each sentence.

1. At age 7, Jane Goodall wanted to _____.
   - Ⓐ talk to animals
   - Ⓑ study chimpanzees
   - Ⓒ go to Africa
   - Ⓓ be a scientist

2. Chimps live in _____.
   - Ⓐ dry deserts
   - Ⓑ sunny grasslands
   - Ⓒ tall mountains
   - Ⓓ dense forests

3. Chimps do <u>not</u> use their language to _____.
   - Ⓐ let others know they have found food
   - Ⓑ show pleasure
   - Ⓒ show alarm
   - Ⓓ tell a story

4. Which of these is <u>not</u> body language?
   - Ⓐ saying "hello" with a hug
   - Ⓑ stomping to show who is in charge
   - Ⓒ barking to warn others
   - Ⓓ tickling a baby to keep it out of trouble

5. Jane Goodall wants others to _____.
   - Ⓐ protect chimps from harm
   - Ⓑ put chimps in zoos
   - Ⓒ cut down the forests chimps live in
   - Ⓓ lead tours through the forests

Bonus: Imagine that you are meeting someone for the first time. On the back of this page, write how you would say "hello" using only body language.

Chimpanzee Champion

For over 30 years, Jane Goodall has been learning about chimpanzees. She has crept and crawled through dense forests in Africa to observe them. She has watched them search for food, play, make friends, and fight. She has learned very important things about them.

Chimps are more closely related to humans than any other animal. Still, it surprised many scientists when Jane learned how much they act like people. She saw chimps using twigs to scoop termites from mounds. That meant they could use tools. Scientists had thought that only humans used tools. Chimps also had social groups like humans. They greeted one another with hugs and kisses. The more Jane watched chimps, the more she thought they were a lot like humans.

Although they act a lot like people, chimps cannot speak for themselves. That's why Jane acts as their champion. She speaks for them. Chimps face many dangers. As people build farms, roads, and houses, they chop down the animals' forest habitats. People hunt chimps for food. They capture chimp infants to sell as pets or lab animals.

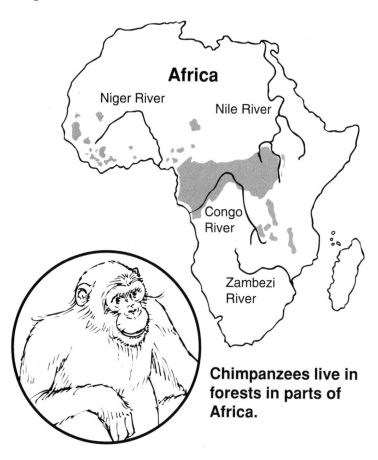

Africa

Niger River

Nile River

Congo River

Zambezi River

Chimpanzees live in forests in parts of Africa.

Because chimps are our closest living relative, Jane thinks they should be protected. She believes that when people harm nature, they also harm themselves. Jane feels that there should be more wildlife sanctuaries in Africa. These protected areas offer safe places for chimps to live. Although chimps face danger every day, she believes that people can work together to make things better.

Name _____

Chimpanzee Champion

Fill in the bubble to answer each question.

1. How long has Jane Goodall been studying chimpanzees?
   - Ⓐ over 10 years
   - Ⓑ over 20 years
   - Ⓒ over 30 years
   - Ⓓ over 40 years

2. Which of these makes chimps like people?
   - Ⓐ Chimps use tools.
   - Ⓑ Chimps go to school.
   - Ⓒ Chimps live in houses.
   - Ⓓ Chimps eat insects.

3. Which of these is a danger that threatens chimps?
   - Ⓐ People go to zoos.
   - Ⓑ People chop down the forests chimps live in.
   - Ⓒ People send money to save the chimps.
   - Ⓓ People make wildlife sanctuaries.

4. Which definition of **sanctuary** best fits this article?
   - Ⓐ an area where animals are protected
   - Ⓑ an area where animals are hunted
   - Ⓒ an area where animals are put in zoos
   - Ⓓ an area where animals are safe from other animals

5. Which word means the opposite of **dense**?
   - Ⓐ thick
   - Ⓑ crowded
   - Ⓒ packed
   - Ⓓ thin

Bonus: Jane Goodall likes to learn about chimpanzees. Choose an animal you would like to learn more about. On the back of this page, write a sentence that tells why you have chosen this animal.

Protecting Your Ears

Introducing the Topic

1. Reproduce page 87 for individual students, or make a transparency to use with a group or your whole class.

2. Present the diagram of the ear, and read the caption and labels to connect the new vocabulary with a graphic representation.

Reading the Selection

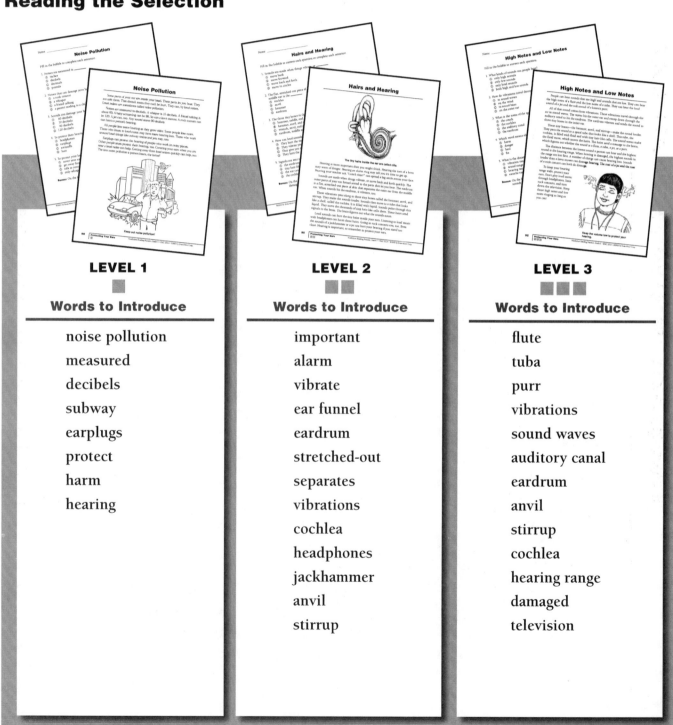

LEVEL 1
■

Words to Introduce

noise pollution

measured

decibels

subway

earplugs

protect

harm

hearing

LEVEL 2
■ ■

Words to Introduce

important

alarm

vibrate

ear funnel

eardrum

stretched-out

separates

vibrations

cochlea

headphones

jackhammer

anvil

stirrup

LEVEL 3
■ ■ ■

Words to Introduce

flute

tuba

purr

vibrations

sound waves

auditory canal

eardrum

anvil

stirrup

cochlea

hearing range

damaged

television

Diagram of the Human Ear

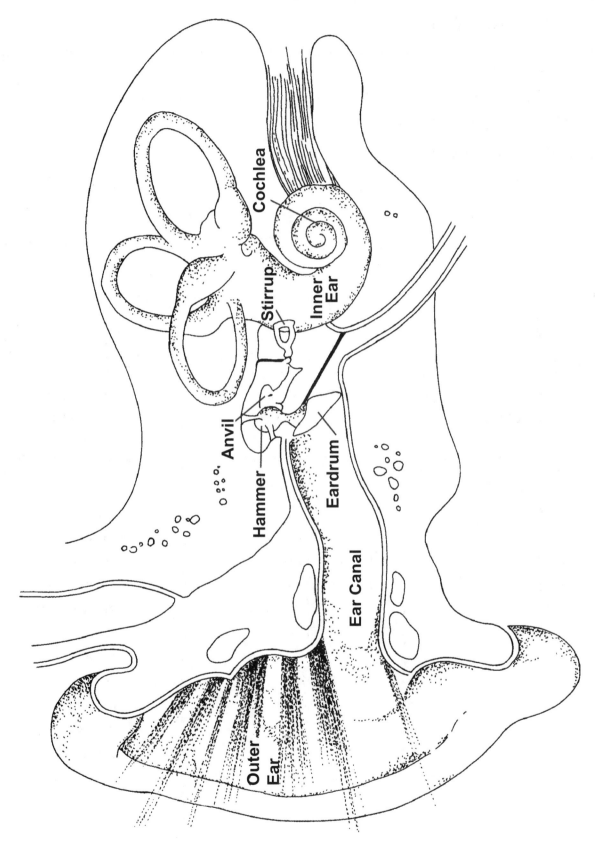

The parts of your ear that let you hear are safe inside your head.

Cochlea
Stirrup
Inner Ear
Anvil
Hammer
Eardrum
Ear Canal
Outer Ear

Noise Pollution

Some parts of your ear are inside your head. These parts let you hear. They are safe there. That doesn't mean they can't be hurt. They can, by loud noises. Loud noises are sometimes called noise pollution.

Noises are measured in decibels. A whisper is 15 decibels. A friend talking is about 60. A baby screaming can be 90. So can a lawn mower. A rock concert can be 120. A jet can, too. Any sound above 90 decibels can harm a person's hearing.

All people lose some hearing as they grow older. Some people lose more. Those who listen to loud music may have more hearing loss. Those who work around loud things like subway trains and jets may, too.

Earplugs can protect the hearing of people who work in noisy places. Other people must protect their hearing, too. Covering your ears when you are near a loud noise can help. Getting away from loud noises quickly can help, too. The less noise pollution a person hears, the better!

Keep out noise pollution!

Name _____

Noise Pollution

Fill in the bubble to complete each sentence.

1. Noises are measured in _____.
   - Ⓐ inches
   - Ⓑ decibels
   - Ⓒ decimals
   - Ⓓ pounds

2. Noises that can damage your hearing include _____.
   - Ⓐ a rock concert
   - Ⓑ a whisper
   - Ⓒ a friend talking
   - Ⓓ a parent reading to a child

3. Sounds can damage your hearing if they are over _____.
   - Ⓐ 60 decibels
   - Ⓑ 70 decibels
   - Ⓒ 90 decibels
   - Ⓓ 120 decibels

4. To protect their hearing, some workers wear _____.
   - Ⓐ headphones
   - Ⓑ earplugs
   - Ⓒ earmuffs
   - Ⓓ hats

5. To protect your hearing, _____.
   - Ⓐ cover your ears when you are near loud noises
   - Ⓑ get away from babies
   - Ⓒ talk to your friends
   - Ⓓ only whisper to people

Bonus: On the back of this page, write one thing you will do to protect your hearing.

Hairs and Hearing

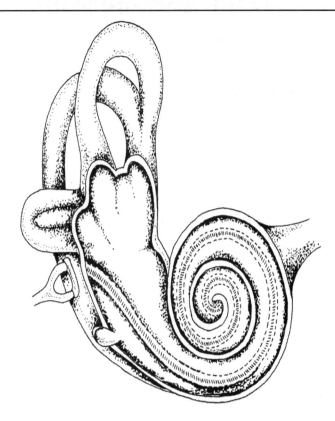

The tiny hairs inside the ear are called cilia.

Hearing is more important than you might think. Hearing the toot of a horn may warn of danger. Hearing an alarm ring may tell you it's time to get up. Hearing your teacher say, "Lunchtime!" can spread a big smile across your face.

Sounds are made when things vibrate, or move back and forth quickly. The outer parts of your ear funnel sound to the parts that let you hear. The eardrum is a flat, stretched-out piece of skin that separates the outer ear from the middle ear. When sounds hit the eardrum, it vibrates, too.

These vibrations pass along to three tiny bones called the hammer, anvil, and stirrup. They make the sounds louder. Sounds then move to a tube that looks like a shell, called the cochlea. It is filled with liquid. Sounds pulse through this liquid. They move the thousands of tiny hair-like cells there. These hairs send signals to the brain. The brain figures out what the sounds mean.

Loud sounds can hurt the tiny hairs inside your ears. Listening to loud music with headphones can harm those hairs. Going to rock concerts can, too. Even the sounds of a jackhammer or a jet can hurt your hearing if you stand too close. Hearing is important, so remember to protect your ears.

Nonfiction Reading Practice, Grade 3 • EMC 3314 • ©2003 by Evan-Moor Corp.

Hairs and Hearing

Fill in the bubble to answer each question or complete each sentence.

1. Sounds are made when things vibrate, or _____.
   - Ⓐ move back
   - Ⓑ move forward
   - Ⓒ move back and forth
   - Ⓓ move in circles

2. The flat, stretched-out piece of skin that separates the outer ear from the middle ear is the _____.
   - Ⓐ cochlea
   - Ⓑ anvil
   - Ⓒ hammer
   - Ⓓ eardrum

3. The three tiny bones in the ear that make sounds louder are the _____.
   - Ⓐ hammer, saddle, and stirrup
   - Ⓑ hammer, anvil, and stirrup
   - Ⓒ wrench, anvil, and stirrup
   - Ⓓ eardrum, middle ear, and outer ear

4. How can loud sounds damage your hearing?
   - Ⓐ They hurt the tiny hairs inside your ears.
   - Ⓑ They vibrate your eardrums.
   - Ⓒ They give you a headache.
   - Ⓓ They hurt the outer ear.

5. Signals are sent to the brain by _____.
   - Ⓐ the eardrum
   - Ⓑ tiny hair-like cells
   - Ⓒ the ear canal
   - Ⓓ the cochlea

Bonus: On the back of this page, make a list of sounds that you think might damage your hearing.

High Notes and Low Notes

People can hear sounds that are high and sounds that are low. They can hear the high notes of a flute and the low notes of a tuba. They can hear the loud sound of a jet and the soft sound of a kitten's purr.

All of that sound comes from vibrations. These vibrations travel through the air in sound waves. The waves hit the outer ear and sweep down through the auditory canal to hit the eardrum. The eardrum vibrates and sends the sound to three tiny bones in the inner ear.

These tiny bones—the hammer, anvil, and stirrup—make the sound louder. They pass the sound to a spiral tube that looks like a shell. This tube, the cochlea, is filled with fluid and tiny hair-like cells. The sound waves make the fluid move, which moves the hairs. The hairs send a message to the brain, which figures out whether the sound is a flute, a tuba, a jet, or a purr.

The distance between the lowest sound a person can hear and the highest sound is the hearing range. When hearing is damaged, the highest sounds in the range are lost first. A number of things can cause hearing loss. Sounds louder than a lawn mower can damage hearing. The roar of a jet and the roar of a rock concert can both do damage.

To keep your hearing range wide, protect your ears. Don't play loud music through headphones, limit rock concerts, and turn down the television. Keep those high notes and low notes ringing as long as you can!

Keep the volume low to protect your hearing.

High Notes and Low Notes

Fill in the bubble to answer each question.

1. What kinds of sounds can people hear?
   - Ⓐ only high sounds
   - Ⓑ only low sounds
   - Ⓒ only loud sounds
   - Ⓓ both high and low sounds

2. How do vibrations travel through the air?
   - Ⓐ in sound waves
   - Ⓑ on the wind
   - Ⓒ in a spiral tube
   - Ⓓ on the outer ear

3. What is the name of the spiral tube in the ear that looks like a shell?
   - Ⓐ the conch
   - Ⓑ the cochlea
   - Ⓒ the auditory canal
   - Ⓓ the eardrum

4. Which word means about the same as **damage**?
   - Ⓐ harm
   - Ⓑ danger
   - Ⓒ heal
   - Ⓓ fix

5. What is the distance between the lowest sound a person can hear and the highest?
   - Ⓐ vibration range
   - Ⓑ sound range
   - Ⓒ hearing range
   - Ⓓ earache range

Bonus: On the back of this page, make a list of three high sounds and three low sounds that you can hear.

In-Line Skating Safety

Introducing the Topic

1. Reproduce page 95 for individual students, or make a transparency to use with a group or your whole class.

2. Present the diagram of the skater, and read the caption and labels to connect the new vocabulary with a graphic representation.

Reading the Selection

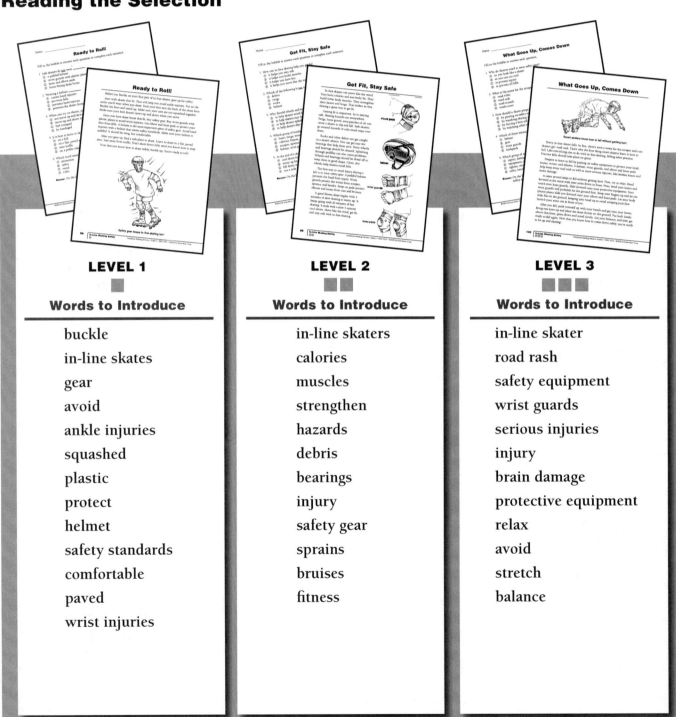

LEVEL 1	**LEVEL 2**	**LEVEL 3**
Words to Introduce	**Words to Introduce**	**Words to Introduce**
buckle	in-line skaters	in-line skater
in-line skates	calories	road rash
gear	muscles	safety equipment
avoid	strengthen	wrist guards
ankle injuries	hazards	serious injuries
squashed	debris	injury
plastic	bearings	brain damage
protect	injury	protective equipment
helmet	safety gear	relax
safety standards	sprains	avoid
comfortable	bruises	stretch
paved	fitness	balance
wrist injuries		

In-Line Skating Safety

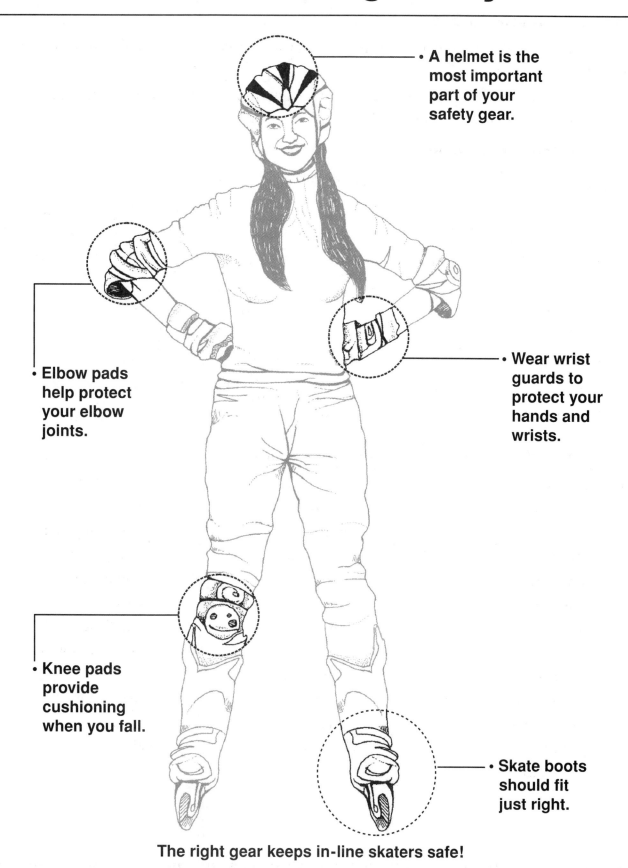

- A helmet is the most important part of your safety gear.

- Wear wrist guards to protect your hands and wrists.

- Elbow pads help protect your elbow joints.

- Knee pads provide cushioning when you fall.

- Skate boots should fit just right.

The right gear keeps in-line skaters safe!

Ready to Roll!

Before you buckle on your first pair of in-line skates, gear up for safety.

Start with skates that fit. That will help you avoid ankle injuries. Put on the socks you'll wear when you skate. Kick your foot into the back of the skate boot. Buckle the boot and stand up. Make sure your toes are not squashed together. Make sure your heel doesn't move up and down when you move.

Once you have skate boots that fit, buy safety gear. Buy wrist guards with plastic plates to avoid wrist injuries. Get elbow and knee pads to protect your skin from falls. A helmet is the most important piece of safety gear. Avoid head injuries with a helmet that meets safety standards. Make sure your helmet is padded. It should be snug, but comfortable.

After you gear up, find a safe place to skate. Learn to skate in a flat, paved area. Stay away from traffic. Don't skate down hills until you know how to stop.

Now that you know how to skate safely, buckle up. You're ready to roll!

Safety gear keeps in-line skating fun!

Name _____

Ready to Roll!

Fill in the bubble to answer each question or complete each sentence.

1. Safe skaters do <u>not</u> wear _____.
   - Ⓐ a padded helmet
   - Ⓑ wrist guards with plastic plates
   - Ⓒ knee and elbow pads
   - Ⓓ loose-fitting skate boots

2. Wearing a helmet _____.
   - Ⓐ causes head injuries
   - Ⓑ prevents falls
   - Ⓒ prevents head injuries
   - Ⓓ prevents the skater from seeing well

3. When you try on skates, your heel should _____.
   - Ⓐ not move up and down in the boot
   - Ⓑ move up and down in the boot
   - Ⓒ feel cramped
   - Ⓓ be bandaged

4. It is best to learn to skate _____.
   - Ⓐ on a hill
   - Ⓑ on a flat, paved area
   - Ⓒ near traffic
   - Ⓓ on a public sidewalk

5. Which word means about the same as **standards**?
   - Ⓐ protection
   - Ⓑ safety
   - Ⓒ stand
   - Ⓓ rules

Bonus: On the back of this page, write three things a safe skater will do.

Get Fit, Stay Safe

In-line skaters can move like the wind. They burn calories and lose body fat. They build lower body muscles. They strengthen their hearts and lungs. That makes in-line skating a great way to get fit.

Getting fit is important. So is staying safe. Skating hazards are everywhere. Twigs, loose gravel, even patches of oil can cause a skater to slip and fall. Safe skaters go around hazards or take small steps over them.

Rocks and other debris can get caught in a skate's wheels. Dirt can get into the bearings that help them turn. Dirty wheels and bearings should be cleaned. Splashing through puddles can also cause problems. Wheels and bearings should be dried off to keep them in good shape. Clean, dry wheels help skaters avoid falls.

The best way to avoid injury during a fall is to wear safety gear. A padded helmet protects the head from injury. Wrist guards protect the wrists from scrapes, sprains, and breaks. Strap-on pads protect elbows and knees from cuts and bruises.

A good fitness skate begins with 5 minutes of slow skating to warm up. It keeps going with 20 minutes of fast skating. It ends with a slow 5-minute cool-down. Move like the wind, get fit, and stay safe with in-line skating.

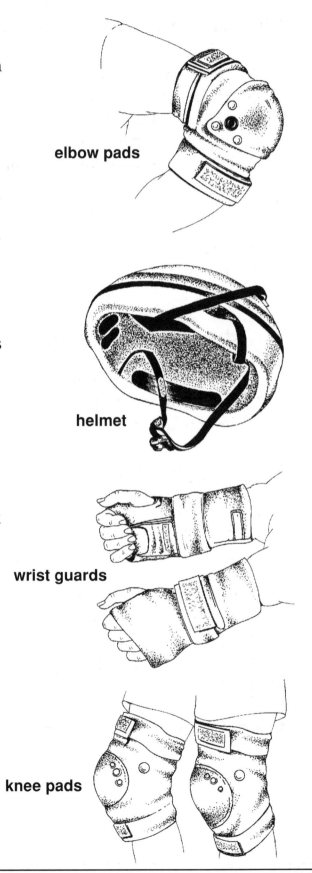

elbow pads

helmet

wrist guards

knee pads

Nonfiction Reading Practice, Grade 3 • EMC 3314 • ©2003 by Evan-Moor Corp.

Name _____

Get Fit, Stay Safe

Fill in the bubble to answer each question or complete each sentence.

1. How can in-line skating help you get fit?
   - Ⓐ It helps you stay safe.
   - Ⓑ It helps you build muscles.
   - Ⓒ It helps you have fun.
   - Ⓓ It helps you move like the wind.

2. Which of the following is <u>not</u> a skating hazard?
   - Ⓐ debris
   - Ⓑ twigs
   - Ⓒ rocks
   - Ⓓ helmet

3. Why should wheels and bearings be clean and dry?
   - Ⓐ to help skaters avoid falls
   - Ⓑ to help skaters stay healthy
   - Ⓒ to help skaters splash through puddles
   - Ⓓ to help skaters slip and fall

4. Which group of words relates to injuries from in-line skating?
   - Ⓐ heart, lungs, muscles
   - Ⓑ calories, fitness, cool-down
   - Ⓒ scrapes, sprains, bruises
   - Ⓓ helmet, wrist guards, elbow pads

5. At the end of a skate, a skater should _____.
   - Ⓐ cool down for 5 minutes
   - Ⓑ warm up for 5 minutes
   - Ⓒ fall down in soft grass
   - Ⓓ run a mile

Bonus: On the back of this page, write a paragraph about what you do to get fit.

What Goes Up, Comes Down

Smart skaters know how to fall without getting hurt.

Every in-line skater falls. In fact, there's even a name for the scrapes and cuts skaters get: road rash. That's why the first thing smart skaters learn is how to fall. Like everything else to do with in-line skating, falling takes practice. Practice falls should take place on grass.

Prepare to learn to fall by putting on safety equipment to protect your head, knees, wrists, and elbows. A helmet, wrist guards, and elbow and knee pads help keep away road rash as well as more serious injuries, like broken bones and brain damage.

It takes several steps to fall without getting hurt. First, try to relax. Bend forward at the waist with your arms down in front. Next, bend your knees and touch your knee guards. Slide forward onto your protective equipment. Your wrist guards will probably hit the ground first. Keep your fingers up and let the plastic plates slide you forward onto your elbow and knee pads. Let your body slide flat on the ground, keeping your head up to avoid scraping your face. Stretch your arms out in front of you.

After you fall, push yourself up with your hands and get onto your knees. Bring one knee up and place the skate firmly on the ground. Put both hands above that knee, press down and stand slowly. Get your balance, and then get ready to fall again. Now that you know how to come down safely, you're ready to be up and skating!

  Nonfiction Reading Practice, Grade 3 • EMC 3314 • ©2003 by Evan-Moor Corp.

Name _____

What Goes Up, Comes Down

Fill in the bubble to answer each question.

1. Why do skaters need to wear safety gear?
   - Ⓐ so you look like a skater
   - Ⓑ so you can act cool
   - Ⓒ to prevent injury
   - Ⓓ to prevent all falls

2. What is the name for the scrapes and cuts that skaters get?
   - Ⓐ road rules
   - Ⓑ road rash
   - Ⓒ road scratch
   - Ⓓ roadrunner

3. Which of these should a skater do first to learn how to fall?
   - Ⓐ by putting on safety equipment
   - Ⓑ by watching skating videos
   - Ⓒ by buying a first-aid kit
   - Ⓓ by watching other skaters fall

4. Which of these means about the same as **equipment**?
   - Ⓐ helmet
   - Ⓑ gear
   - Ⓒ wrist guards
   - Ⓓ backpack

5. Which group of words relates to how a skater should fall?
   - Ⓐ injury, damage, road rash
   - Ⓑ equipment, plastic, brain
   - Ⓒ tighten, straighten, jump
   - Ⓓ relax, bend, slide

Bonus: On the back of this page, draw a picture of yourself wearing in-line skating safety equipment.

Dr. Edward Jenner

Introducing the Topic

1. Reproduce page 103 for individual students, or make a transparency to use with a group or your whole class.

2. Present the drawing of Dr. Edward Jenner, and read the caption to connect the new vocabulary with a graphic representation.

Reading the Selection

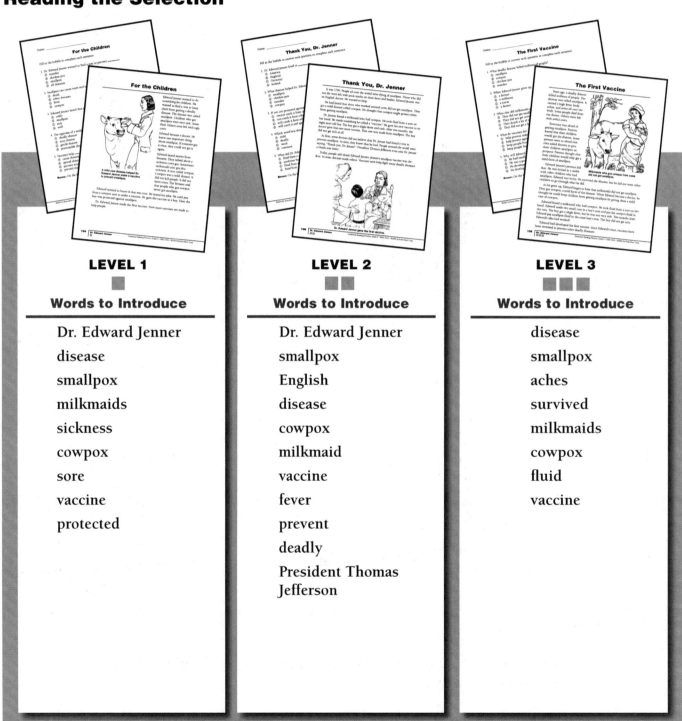

LEVEL 1

Words to Introduce

Dr. Edward Jenner

disease

smallpox

milkmaids

sickness

cowpox

sore

vaccine

protected

LEVEL 2

Words to Introduce

Dr. Edward Jenner

smallpox

English

disease

cowpox

milkmaid

vaccine

fever

prevent

deadly

President Thomas Jefferson

LEVEL 3

Words to Introduce

disease

smallpox

aches

survived

milkmaids

cowpox

fluid

vaccine

Nonfiction Reading Practice, Grade 3 • EMC 3314 • ©2003 by Evan-Moor Corp.

Dr. Edward Jenner

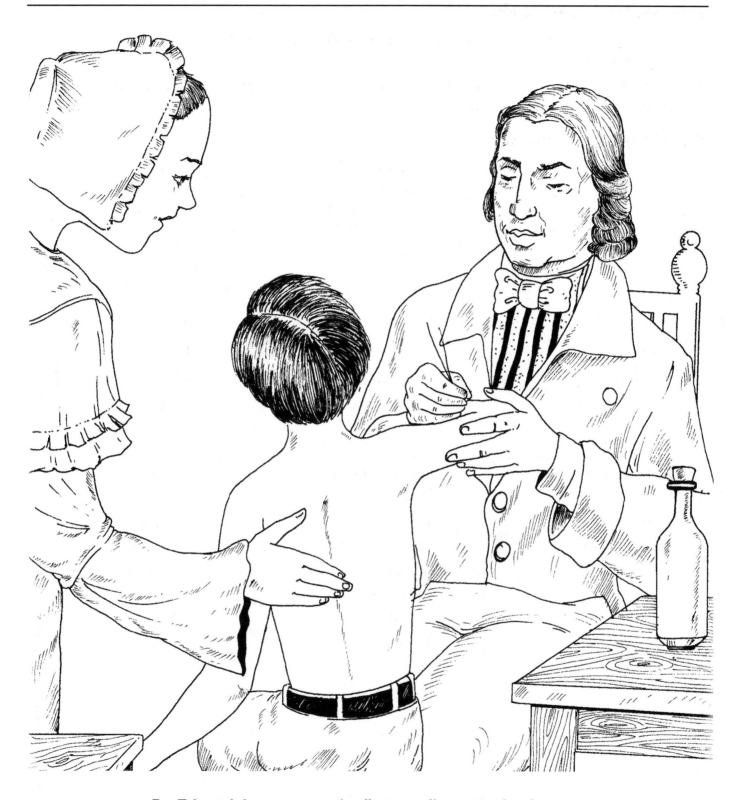

Dr. Edward Jenner gave the first smallpox vaccination to an eight-year-old boy.

For the Children

A mild cow disease helped Dr. Edward Jenner make a vaccine to prevent smallpox.

Edward Jenner wanted to do something for children. He wanted to find a way to keep them from getting a deadly disease. The disease was called smallpox. Children who got smallpox were very sick. Some died. Others were left with ugly scars.

Edward became a doctor. He knew one important thing about smallpox. If someone got it once, they could not get it again.

Edward heard stories from farmers. They talked about a sickness cows got. Sometimes milkmaids also got this sickness. It was called cowpox. Cowpox was a mild disease. It did not kill people. It did not leave scars. The farmers said that people who got cowpox never got smallpox.

Edward wanted to know if that was true. He tested his idea. He used pus from a cowpox sore to make a vaccine. He gave the vaccine to a boy. Then the boy was protected against smallpox.

Dr. Edward Jenner made the first vaccine. Now more vaccines are made to help people.

Nonfiction Reading Practice, Grade 3 • EMC 3314 • ©2003 by Evan-Moor Corp.

Name _____

For the Children

Fill in the bubble to complete each sentence.

1. Dr. Edward Jenner wanted to find a way to prevent _____.
   - Ⓐ measles
   - Ⓑ chicken pox
   - Ⓒ smallpox
   - Ⓓ all diseases

2. Smallpox can cause scars and sometimes _____.
   - Ⓐ death
   - Ⓑ other diseases
   - Ⓒ fever
   - Ⓓ cowpox

3. Edward Jenner heard that people who got cowpox did not get _____.
   - Ⓐ colds
   - Ⓑ smallpox
   - Ⓒ sick
   - Ⓓ well

4. The opposite of a **mild disease** is _____.
   - Ⓐ a deadly disease
   - Ⓑ an easy disease
   - Ⓒ a gentle disease
   - Ⓓ a preventable disease

5. Vaccines help _____.
   - Ⓐ cause disease
   - Ⓑ spread disease
   - Ⓒ prevent scarring
   - Ⓓ prevent disease

Bonus: On the back of this page, write three facts about Dr. Edward Jenner.

Thank You, Dr. Jenner

It was 1796. People all over the world were dying of smallpox. Those who did not die were left with pock marks on their faces and bodies. Edward Jenner was an English doctor. He wanted to help.

He had heard that those who worked around cows did not get smallpox. They got a mild disease called cowpox. He thought that cowpox might protect them from getting smallpox.

Dr. Jenner found a milkmaid who had cowpox. He took fluid from a sore on her hand. He made something he called a "vaccine." He gave his new vaccine to an eight-year-old boy. The boy got a slight fever and rash. After two months, the doctor gave him one more vaccine. This one was made from smallpox. The boy did not get sick at all.

At first, some doctors did not believe that Dr. Jenner had found a way to prevent smallpox. In time, they knew that he had. People around the world were saying, "Thank you, Dr. Jenner!" President Thomas Jefferson even sent Dr. Jenner a thank-you letter.

Today, people still thank Edward Jenner. Jenner's smallpox vaccine was the first. In time, doctors made others. Vaccines now help fight many deadly diseases.

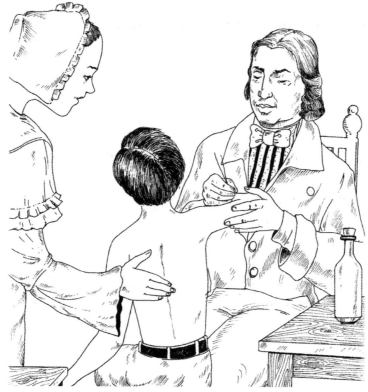

Dr. Edward Jenner gave the first vaccine.

Nonfiction Reading Practice, Grade 3 • EMC 3314 • ©2003 by Evan-Moor Corp.

Name _____

Thank You, Dr. Jenner

Fill in the bubble to answer each question or complete each sentence.

1. Dr. Edward Jenner lived in _____.
   - Ⓐ America
   - Ⓑ England
   - Ⓒ Germany
   - Ⓓ Ireland

2. Which disease helped Dr. Edward Jenner make his vaccine?
   - Ⓐ smallpox
   - Ⓑ chicken pox
   - Ⓒ measles
   - Ⓓ cowpox

3. If you are **protected** against a disease, you _____.
   - Ⓐ cannot catch it from others
   - Ⓑ can catch it from others
   - Ⓒ will catch it from others
   - Ⓓ will catch it and spread it to others

4. Which word best describes the disease **smallpox**?
   - Ⓐ mild
   - Ⓑ deadly
   - Ⓒ weak
   - Ⓓ common

5. What did Dr. Edward Jenner use to vaccinate the boy against smallpox?
   - Ⓐ fluid from a cow
   - Ⓑ medicine from a drugstore
   - Ⓒ fluid from a cowpox sore
   - Ⓓ fluid from a smallpox sore

Bonus: On the back of this page, write a thank-you note to Dr. Edward Jenner.

The First Vaccine

Years ago, a deadly disease killed millions of people. The disease was called smallpox. It caused a high fever, body aches, and sores all over the body. Some people died from the disease. Others were left with awful scars.

Everyone was afraid of getting smallpox. Parents feared that their children would get the disease. Some parents were so afraid that they asked doctors to give their children smallpox on purpose. Parents thought that their children would only get a mild form of smallpox.

Edward Jenner's parents did that. He was locked in a stable with other children who had

Milkmaids who got cowpox from cows did not get smallpox.

smallpox. Edward was lucky. He survived the disease, but he did not want other children to go through what he did.

As he grew up, Edward began to hear that milkmaids did not get smallpox. They got cowpox, a mild form of the disease. When Edward became a doctor, he thought he could keep children from getting smallpox by giving them a mild case of cowpox.

Edward found a milkmaid who had cowpox. He took fluid from a sore on her hand. Edward made two small cuts in a boy's arm and put the cowpox fluid in the cuts. The boy got a slight fever, but he was not very sick. Two months later, Edward put smallpox fluid in the same boy's arm. The boy did not get sick. Edward's idea had worked!

Edward had developed the first vaccine. Since Edward's time, vaccines have been invented to prevent other deadly diseases.

Name _____

The First Vaccine

Fill in the bubble to answer each question or complete each sentence.

1. What deadly disease killed millions of people?
   Ⓐ smallpox
   Ⓑ cowpox
   Ⓒ chicken pox
   Ⓓ measles

2. When Edward Jenner grew up, he became _____.
   Ⓐ a farmer
   Ⓑ a milkman
   Ⓒ a nurse
   Ⓓ a doctor

3. What clue did milkmaids give Dr. Jenner that helped him make his vaccine?
   Ⓐ They did not get smallpox.
   Ⓑ They did not get cowpox.
   Ⓒ They drank a lot of milk.
   Ⓓ They did not get a fever.

4. What do vaccines do?
   Ⓐ help prevent rashes
   Ⓑ help protect against disease
   Ⓒ keep people from catching colds
   Ⓓ keep people from going to the doctor

5. Why will Edward Jenner always be remembered?
   Ⓐ He had smallpox as a child.
   Ⓑ He was a good doctor.
   Ⓒ He developed the first vaccine.
   Ⓓ He developed many vaccines.

Bonus: On the back of this page, write four facts about smallpox.

Gold Medal Numbers

Introducing the Topic

1. Reproduce page 111 for individual students, or make a transparency to use with a group or your whole class.

2. Present the drawing of timing devices, and read the captions to connect the new vocabulary with a graphic representation.

Reading the Selection

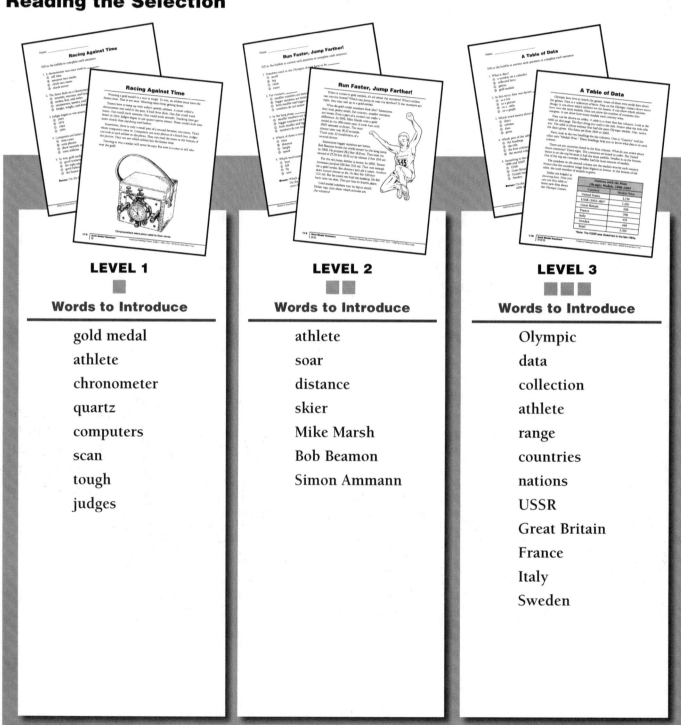

LEVEL 1
■

Words to Introduce

gold medal

athlete

chronometer

quartz

computers

scan

tough

judges

LEVEL 2
■ ■

Words to Introduce

athlete

soar

distance

skier

Mike Marsh

Bob Beamon

Simon Ammann

LEVEL 3
■ ■ ■

Words to Introduce

Olympic

data

collection

athlete

range

countries

nations

USSR

Great Britain

France

Italy

Sweden

Timing Instruments

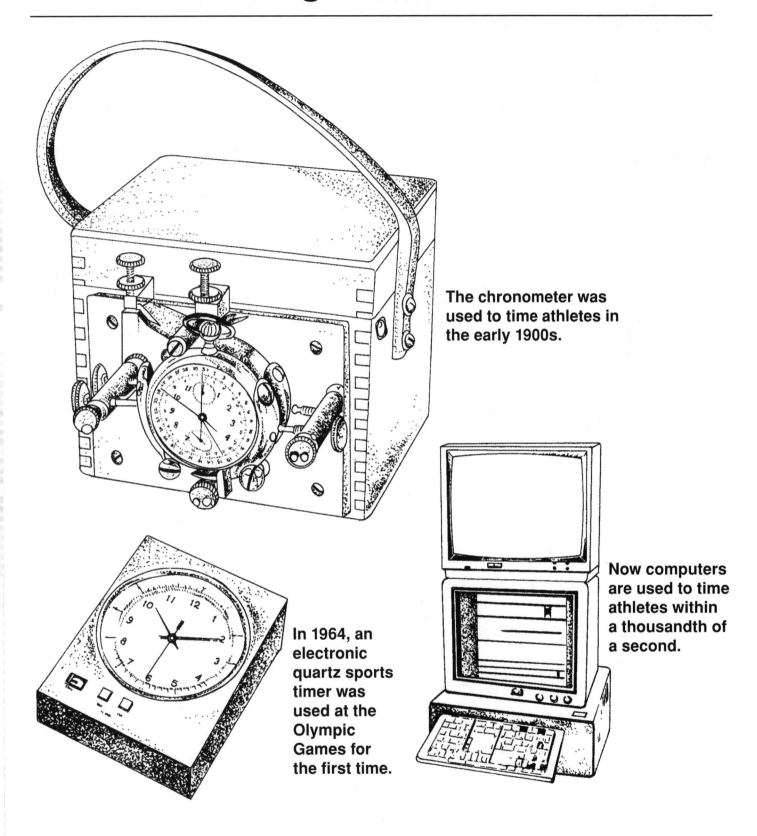

The chronometer was used to time athletes in the early 1900s.

In 1964, an electronic quartz sports timer was used at the Olympic Games for the first time.

Now computers are used to time athletes within a thousandth of a second.

Racing Against Time

Winning a gold medal in a race is tough. To win, an athlete must have the fastest time. That is not easy. Winning times keep getting faster.

Timers have to keep up with today's speedy athletes. A timer called a chronometer was used in the past. It had three dials. One dial could track hours. One could track minutes. One could track seconds. Tracking time got better in 1964. Judges began to use quartz sports timers. These could clock time more closely than anything used before.

Sometimes, there is only a small part of a second between two times. That's where computers come in. Computers can scan photos of a finish line. Judges can look at each athlete in the photo. They can read the times at the bottom of the picture. They can see which athlete has the fastest time.

Training to win a medal will never be easy. But now it is easy to tell who won the gold!

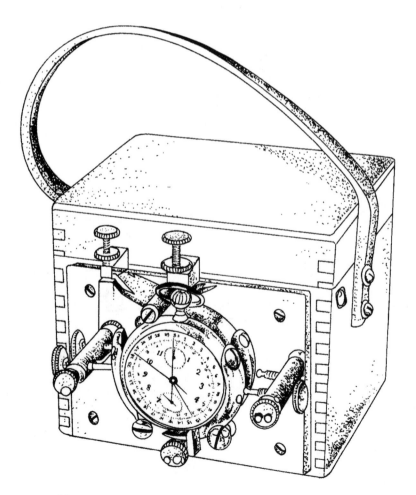

Chronometers were once used to time races.

Nonfiction Reading Practice, Grade 3 • EMC 3314 • ©2003 by Evan-Moor Corp.

Name _____

Racing Against Time

Fill in the bubble to complete each sentence.

1. A chronometer was once used to _____.
   - Ⓐ tell time
   - Ⓑ measure race tracks
   - Ⓒ clock race times
   - Ⓓ check scores

2. The three dials on a chronometer measured _____.
   - Ⓐ seconds, minutes, and hours
   - Ⓑ inches, feet, and miles
   - Ⓒ centimeters, meters, and kilometers
   - Ⓓ height, weight, and distance

3. Judges began to use quartz sports timers in _____.
   - Ⓐ 1964
   - Ⓑ 1974
   - Ⓒ 1984
   - Ⓓ 1994

4. Computers are better than quartz sports timers because they can _____.
   - Ⓐ time races
   - Ⓑ scan photos
   - Ⓒ show seconds on the clock
   - Ⓓ train athletes

5. To win, gold medal racers must have _____.
   - Ⓐ good trainers
   - Ⓑ the right equipment
   - Ⓒ good balance
   - Ⓓ the fastest time

Bonus: On the back of this page, write a sentence about your favorite kind of race.

Run Faster, Jump Farther!

When it comes to gold medals, it's all about the numbers! Which athlete can run the fastest? Which can jump or soar the farthest? If the numbers are right, they may add up to a gold medal.

What do gold medal numbers look like? Sometimes they look pretty small. For runners, smaller numbers are better. Even a part of a second can make a difference. In 1992, Mike Marsh won a gold medal in the 200-meter race. It took him only 20.01 seconds to finish. The next closest time was 20.13 seconds. That's only 12 hundredths of a second slower.

Sometimes bigger numbers are better. Bob Beamon broke the world record in the long jump in 1968. He jumped 29.2 feet (8.9 m). That beat the record of 27.39 feet (8.35 m) by almost 2 feet (0.6 m).

For the ski jump, farther is better. In 2002, Simon Ammann jumped 436 feet (133 m). That was enough for a gold medal. But distance isn't all it takes. Another skier soared almost as far. He flew for 430 feet (131 m). But he could not hold his landing. He fell back onto his skis. That put him in fourth place.

Gold medal numbers may be big or small. Either way, they show which athletes are the winners!

Gold Medal Numbers   Nonfiction Reading Practice, Grade 3 • EMC 3314 • ©2003 by Evan-Moor Corp.

Name _____

Run Faster, Jump Farther!

Fill in the bubble to answer each question or complete each sentence.

1. Numbers used in the Olympics always have to be _____.
   - Ⓐ small
   - Ⓑ big
   - Ⓒ close
   - Ⓓ exact

2. For runners, _____.
   - Ⓐ smaller numbers are better
   - Ⓑ bigger numbers are better
   - Ⓒ both smaller and bigger numbers are needed
   - Ⓓ numbers do not matter

3. In the long jump, _____.
   - Ⓐ smaller numbers are better
   - Ⓑ bigger numbers are better
   - Ⓒ both smaller and bigger numbers are needed
   - Ⓓ numbers do not matter

4. Which of these is most important in the ski jump?
   - Ⓐ time
   - Ⓑ distance
   - Ⓒ height
   - Ⓓ speed

5. Which word means about the same as **soar**?
   - Ⓐ hurt
   - Ⓑ fall
   - Ⓒ fly
   - Ⓓ sore

Bonus: Which gold medal winner in this article would you most like to be? On the back of this page, write a paragraph naming and explaining your choice.

A Table of Data

Olympic fans love to watch the games. Some of them even study data about the games. Data is a collection of facts. Data on the Olympic Games shows many things. It can show which athletes are the fastest. It can show which athletes have won the most medals. Data can show the number of countries that compete. It can show how many medals each country wins.

Data can be shown on tables. A table is a chart that has columns. Look at the table on this page. The first thing you read is the title. Notice what the title tells you. The table is about nations that had the most Olympic medals. Also, notice the dates given. The dates are from 1896 to 2000.

Next, look at the two headings for the columns. One is "Country" and the other says "Medals Won." These headings help you to know what data is in each column.

There are six countries listed in the first column. What do you notice about those countries? That's right. The countries are listed in order. The United States is on the top because it had the most medals. Sweden is on the bottom. Out of the top six countries, Sweden had the fewest number of medals.

The numbers in the second column are the medals won by each country. Notice that the numbers range from highest to lowest. At the bottom of the table, the total number of medals is given.

Tables are helpful in showing data. Now you can use this table to learn new data about the Olympic Games.

Nations with the Most Olympic Medals, 1896–2000	
Country	Medals Won
United States	2,116
USSR (1952–88)*	1,010
Great Britain	638
France	598
Italy	479
Sweden	469
Total	5,310

*Note: The USSR was dissolved in the late 1980s.

Name _____

A Table of Data

Fill in the bubble to answer each question or complete each sentence.

1. What is data?
   - Ⓐ a number on a calendar
   - Ⓑ collected facts
   - Ⓒ games
   - Ⓓ gold medals

2. In this article, data was shown _____.
   - Ⓐ as a list
   - Ⓑ as a picture
   - Ⓒ on a table
   - Ⓓ on a graph

3. Which word means about the same as **table**?
   - Ⓐ chart
   - Ⓑ column
   - Ⓒ data
   - Ⓓ game

4. Which part of the table should you read first?
   - Ⓐ the headings
   - Ⓑ the title
   - Ⓒ the first column
   - Ⓓ the second column

5. According to the table on page 116, which nation won the most medals between 1896 and 2000?
   - Ⓐ USSR
   - Ⓑ Great Britain
   - Ⓒ United States
   - Ⓓ Sweden

Bonus: On the back of this page, make up a math problem using the data in the table on page 116. Be sure to include the answer.

Calendars in History

Introducing the Topic

1. Reproduce page 119 for individual students, or make a transparency to use with a group or your whole class.

2. Present the diagram of the calendar, and read the caption and labels to connect the new vocabulary with a graphic representation.

Reading the Selection

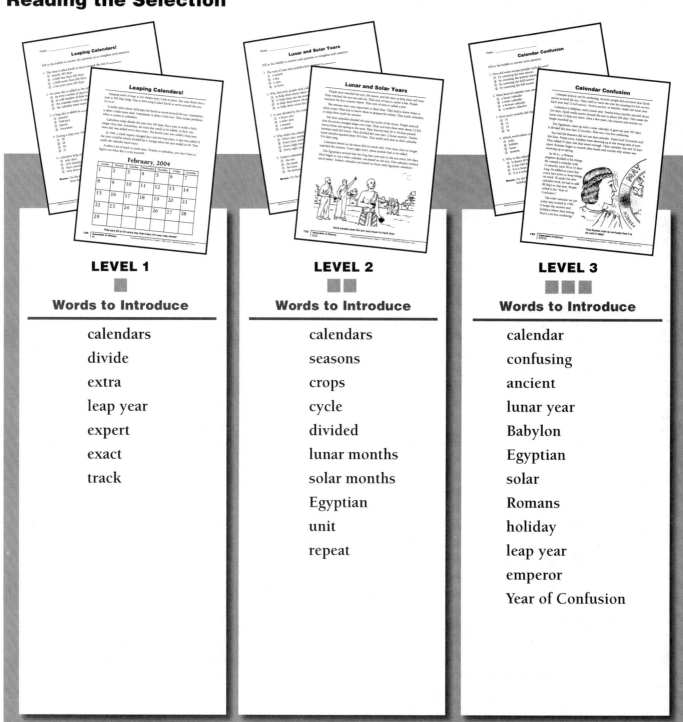

LEVEL 1
■

Words to Introduce

calendars

divide

extra

leap year

expert

exact

track

LEVEL 2
■ ■

Words to Introduce

calendars

seasons

crops

cycle

divided

lunar months

solar months

Egyptian

unit

repeat

LEVEL 3
■ ■ ■

Words to Introduce

calendar

confusing

ancient

lunar year

Babylon

Egyptian

solar

Romans

holiday

leap year

emperor

Year of Confusion

A Modern Calendar

day →
month →
January 2003
year →
date →

Sunday	Monday	Tuesday	Wednesday	Thursday	Friday	Saturday
			1	2	3	4
5	6	7	8	9	10	11
12	13	14	15	16	17	18
19	20	21	22	23	24	25
26	27	28	29	30	31	

Today's calendars help us keep track of years, months, days, and dates.

Leaping Calendars!

Keeping track of time is not always easy. Look at years. You may think that a year is 365 days long. That is how long it takes Earth to move around the sun. Or is it?

It really takes about $365\frac{1}{4}$ days for Earth to move around the sun. Sometimes, it takes a little more time. Sometimes, it takes a little less. That causes problems when it comes to calendars.

Calendars today divide the year into 365 days. But a year is really a little longer than that. Sometimes, an extra day needs to be added. At first, the extra day was added every four years. The fourth year was called a leap year.

In 1582, a math expert changed the rules for leap years. A day was added if the year could be evenly divided by 4, except when the year ended in 00. That made the calendar more exact.

It takes a lot of math to track time. Thanks to calendars, you don't have to figure out what day it is by yourself.

February 2004

Sunday	Monday	Tuesday	Wednesday	Thursday	Friday	Saturday
1	2	3	4	5	6	7
8	9	10	11	12	13	14
15	16	17	18	19	20	21
22	23	24	25	26	27	28
29						

February 29 is the extra day that helps the year leap ahead!

Name _____

Leaping Calendars!

Fill in the bubble to answer the question or to complete each sentence.

1. The time it takes Earth to move around the sun is _____.
   - Ⓐ exactly 365 days
   - Ⓑ a little less than 365 days
   - Ⓒ a little more than 365 days
   - Ⓓ a lot more than 365 days

2. An extra day is added to the calendar every four years to make _____.
   - Ⓐ an even number of days in a month
   - Ⓑ an odd number of days in a month
   - Ⓒ the calendar easier to read
   - Ⓓ the calendar more exact

3. A leap day is added in _____.
   - Ⓐ January
   - Ⓑ February
   - Ⓒ March
   - Ⓓ December

4. During a leap year, February has how many days?
   - Ⓐ 29
   - Ⓑ 28
   - Ⓒ 30
   - Ⓓ 31

5. Calendars help you figure out _____.
   - Ⓐ only days
   - Ⓑ only months
   - Ⓒ days, months, and years
   - Ⓓ only days and months

Bonus: On the back of this page, write a sentence telling what calendar date is most important to you and why.

Lunar and Solar Years

People once watched the sun, the moon, and the stars to help them tell time. They watched the sun rise and set. That unit of time is called a day. People watched the four seasons repeat. That unit of time is called a year.

The seasons were very important to their lives. They had to know when to plant crops. They had to know when to prepare for winter. They made calendars to help them track the seasons.

The first calendars divided the year by cycles of the moon. People noticed that the moon changed shape over time. They saw that there were about 12 full moons from one spring to the next. They learned that 29 or 30 days passed between each full moon. They divided the year into 12 lunar months. Twelve lunar months equaled about 354 days. That made each year in their calendar 354 days long.

Calendars based on the moon did not work well. Over time, they no longer matched the seasons. Every eight years, three months had to be added.

The Egyptians noticed that the Dog Star rose next to the sun every 365 days. They began to use a solar calendar, one based on the sun. This calendar worked much better. Today's calendars are based on those early Egyptian calendars.

Early people used the sun and the moon to track time.

Nonfiction Reading Practice, Grade 3 • EMC 3314 • ©2003 by Evan-Moor Corp.

Name _____

Lunar and Solar Years

Fill in the bubble to answer each question or complete each sentence.

1. The unit of time that includes four seasons is _____.
   - Ⓐ a month
   - Ⓑ a day
   - Ⓒ a year
   - Ⓓ an hour

2. Why did early people need calendars?
   - Ⓐ to help them know when to plant crops
   - Ⓑ to help them see the moon changing
   - Ⓒ to help them know when to prepare for dinner
   - Ⓓ to help them count the number of stars

3. A year divided by the cycles of the moon is _____.
   - Ⓐ a lunar year
   - Ⓑ a solar year
   - Ⓒ a season
   - Ⓓ a calendar

4. Why didn't the calendar that was based on the moon work very well?
   - Ⓐ Every year, another day had to be added.
   - Ⓑ Every year, another month had to be added.
   - Ⓒ Every eight years, three months had to be added.
   - Ⓓ Every eight years, three months had to be subtracted.

5. Today's calendars are based on _____.
   - Ⓐ the sun
   - Ⓑ the moon
   - Ⓒ the stars
   - Ⓓ the seasons

Bonus: On the back of this page, write four facts about calendar history.

Calendar Confusion

Calendar history can be confusing. Ancient people did not know that Earth moves around the sun. They tried to track the year by counting the full moons. Each year had 12 full moons. Twelve moons, or months, made one lunar year.

Calendars in Babylon used a lunar year. Twelve lunar months equaled about 354 days. Earth really moves around the sun in about 365 days. That made the lunar year 11 days too short. After a few years, the seasons and months no longer matched up.

The Egyptians came up with a solar calendar. It gave the year 365 days. It divided the year into 12 months. That was a lot less confusing.

Too bad the Romans did not use that calendar. Theirs had 10 months and 304 days. Pretty soon, holidays were showing up at the wrong time of year. They added 51 days, but that wasn't enough. Their calendar was still 10 days short. Romans began to scratch their heads and wonder why winter was showing up in spring.

In 46 B.C., a Roman emperor decided to fix things. He created a calendar with 12 months, each 30 or 31 days long. He added an extra day every four years to keep things on track. To make his new calendar work, he had to add 80 days to that year. People called it the "Year of Confusion."

The solar calendar we use today was created in 1582. It keeps the seasons and holidays where they belong. That's a lot less confusing!

This Roman man is confused that it is so cold in May!

Nonfiction Reading Practice, Grade 3 • EMC 3314 • ©2003 by Evan-Moor Corp.

Name _____

Calendar Confusion

Fill in the bubble to answer each question.

1. How did some ancient people track the year?
   - Ⓐ by counting the new moons
   - Ⓑ by counting the quarter moons
   - Ⓒ by counting the half moons
   - Ⓓ by counting the full moons

2. What kind of calendar was used in Babylon?
   - Ⓐ a lunar calendar
   - Ⓑ a solar calendar
   - Ⓒ a Roman calendar
   - Ⓓ a modern calendar

3. How many months did the Roman calendar have before 46 B.C.?
   - Ⓐ 10
   - Ⓑ 12
   - Ⓒ 14
   - Ⓓ 16

4. Which word relates to the moon?
   - Ⓐ solar
   - Ⓑ holiday
   - Ⓒ lunar
   - Ⓓ seasons

5. Why is the calendar we use today better than some ancient calendars?
   - Ⓐ It shows all five seasons.
   - Ⓑ It has 365 days, plus an extra day in a leap year.
   - Ⓒ It is a lunar calendar.
   - Ⓓ It is a solar calendar.

Bonus: On the back of this page, write a paragraph about how your favorite holiday would change if it fell in the wrong season.

Tessellations

Introducing the Topic

1. Reproduce page 127 for individual students, or make a transparency to use with a group or your whole class.

2. Present the diagram of the statue, and read the caption to connect the new vocabulary with a graphic representation.

Reading the Selection

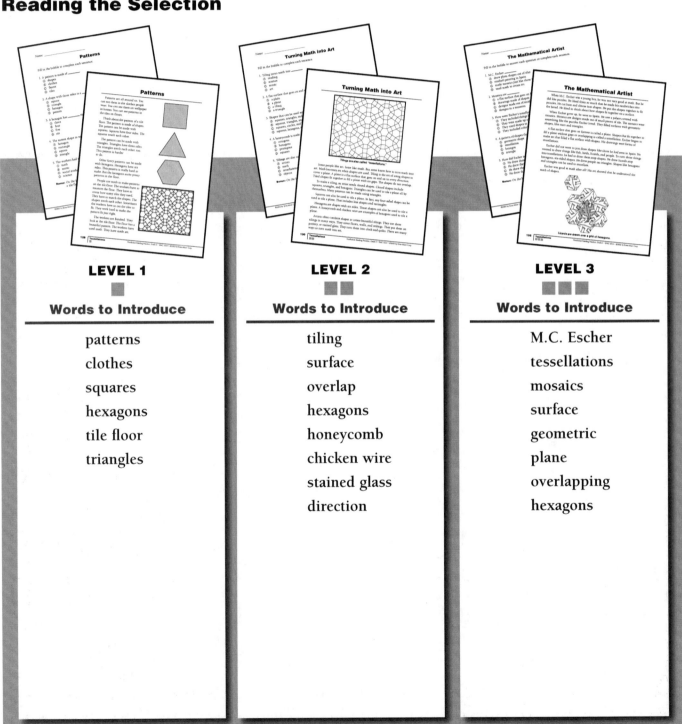

LEVEL 1

Words to Introduce

patterns

clothes

squares

hexagons

tile floor

triangles

LEVEL 2

Words to Introduce

tiling

surface

overlap

hexagons

honeycomb

chicken wire

stained glass

direction

LEVEL 3

Words to Introduce

M.C. Escher

tessellations

mosaics

surface

geometric

plane

overlapping

hexagons

Nonfiction Reading Practice, Grade 3 • EMC 3314 • ©2003 by Evan-Moor Corp.

Tessellations

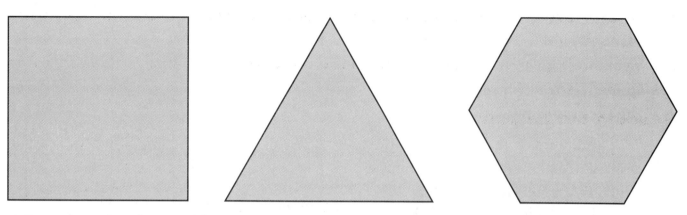

Squares, triangles, and hexagons are shapes that can be used to make tessellations.

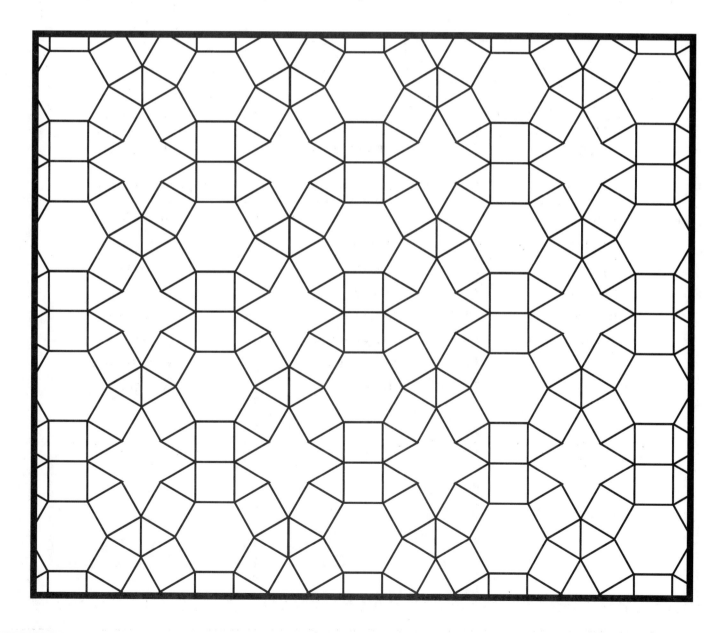

Patterns

Patterns are all around us. You can see them in the clothes people wear. You can see them on wallpaper in homes. You can see patterns in the tiles on floors.

Think about the pattern of a tile floor. The pattern is made of shapes. The pattern can be made with squares. Squares have four sides. The squares touch each other.

The pattern can be made with triangles. Triangles have three sides. The triangles touch each other, too. This pattern is harder to do.

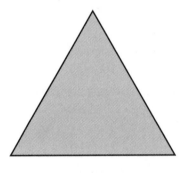

Other fancy patterns can be made with hexagons. Hexagons have six sides. This pattern is really hard to make. But the hexagons make pretty patterns in the floor.

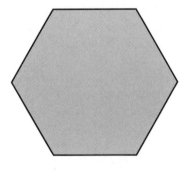

People use math to make patterns on the tile floor. The workers have to measure the floor. They have to count how many tiles they need. They have to match the shapes. The shapes touch each other. Sometimes the workers have to cut the tiles to fit. They work hard to make the pattern fit just right.

The workers are finished. They look at the tile floor. The floor has a beautiful pattern. The workers have used math. They have made art.

Nonfiction Reading Practice, Grade 3 • EMC 3314 • ©2003 by Evan-Moor Corp.

Name _____

Patterns

Fill in the bubble to complete each sentence.

1. A pattern is made of _____.
   - Ⓐ shapes
   - Ⓑ clothes
   - Ⓒ floors
   - Ⓓ tiles

2. A shape with three sides is _____.
   - Ⓐ a square
   - Ⓑ a triangle
   - Ⓒ a hexagon
   - Ⓓ a pattern

3. A hexagon has _____ sides.
   - Ⓐ three
   - Ⓑ four
   - Ⓒ five
   - Ⓓ six

4. The easiest shape to use to make a pattern on a tile floor is _____.
   - Ⓐ a hexagon
   - Ⓑ a rectangle
   - Ⓒ a square
   - Ⓓ a triangle

5. The workers had to use _____ to make the tile floor.
   - Ⓐ math
   - Ⓑ music
   - Ⓒ social studies
   - Ⓓ science

Bonus: On the back of this page, write about how workers use math to make a tile floor.

Turning Math into Art

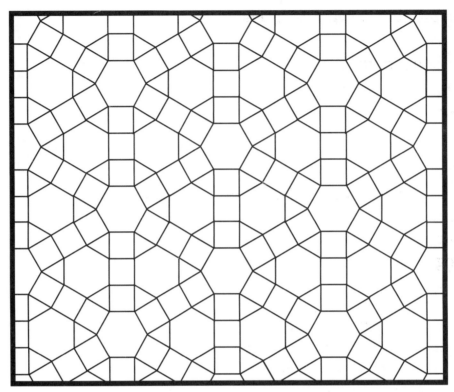

Tilings are also called "tessellations."

Some people like art. Some like math. But some know how to turn math into art. Math becomes art when shapes are used. Tiling is the art of using shapes to cover a plane. A plane is a flat surface that goes on and on in every direction. Tiled shapes fit together to fill a plane with no gaps. The shapes do not overlap.

To make a tiling, an artist needs closed shapes. Closed shapes include squares, triangles, and hexagons. Triangles can be used to tile a plane all by themselves. Many patterns can be made using triangles.

Squares can also be used to tile a plane. In fact, any four-sided shape can be used to tile a plane. That includes kite shapes and rectangles.

Hexagons are shapes with six sides. These shapes can also be used to tile a plane. A honeycomb and chicken wire are examples of hexagons used to tile a plane.

Artists often combine shapes to create beautiful tilings. They use these tilings in many ways. They cover floors, walls, and ceilings. They put them on pottery or stained glass. They turn them into cloth and quilts. There are many ways to turn math into art.

Nonfiction Reading Practice, Grade 3 • EMC 3314 • ©2003 by Evan-Moor Corp.

Name _____

Turning Math into Art

Fill in the bubble to complete each sentence.

1. Tiling turns math into _____.
   - Ⓐ reading
   - Ⓑ science
   - Ⓒ music
   - Ⓓ art

2. A flat surface that goes on and on in every direction is _____.
   - Ⓐ a plain
   - Ⓑ a plane
   - Ⓒ a tiling
   - Ⓓ a triangle

3. Shapes that can be used separately to tile a plane include _____.
   - Ⓐ squares, triangles, and hexagons
   - Ⓑ squares, triangles, and circles
   - Ⓒ squares, circles, and hexagons
   - Ⓓ squares, hexagons, and ovals

4. A honeycomb is made up of _____.
   - Ⓐ octagons
   - Ⓑ hexagons
   - Ⓒ pentagons
   - Ⓓ squares

5. **Tilings** are also called _____.
   - Ⓐ artists
   - Ⓑ math
   - Ⓒ tessellations
   - Ⓓ objects

Bonus: On the back of this page, write four facts about tilings.

The Mathematical Artist

When M.C. Escher was a young boy, he was not very good at math. But he did like puzzles. He liked them so much that he made his sandwiches into puzzles. He cut ham and cheese into shapes. He put the shapes together to fit the bread. He liked to think about how shapes fit together on a surface.

When Escher grew up, he went to Spain. He saw a palace covered with mosaics. Mosaics are designs made out of small pieces of tile. The mosaics were something like the puzzles Escher loved. They filled surfaces with geometric shapes, like stars and triangles.

A flat surface that goes on forever is called a plane. Shapes that fit together to fill a plane without gaps or overlapping is called a tessellation. Escher began to make art that filled a flat surface with shapes. His drawings were forms of tessellations.

Escher did not want to just draw shapes like those he had seen in Spain. He wanted to draw things like fish, birds, lizards, and people. To turn those things into tessellations, he had to draw them atop shapes. He drew lizards atop hexagons, or six-sided shapes. He drew people on triangles. Shapes like hexagons and triangles can be used to tessellate.

Escher was good at math after all! His art showed that he understood the math of shapes.

Lizards are drawn over a grid of hexagons.

Nonfiction Reading Practice, Grade 3 • EMC 3314 • ©2003 by Evan-Moor Corp.

Name _____

The Mathematical Artist

Fill in the bubble to answer each question or complete each sentence.

1. M.C. Escher _____.
   - Ⓐ drew plain shapes out of tiles
   - Ⓑ studied painting in Spain
   - Ⓒ made palaces just like those in Spain
   - Ⓓ used math to create art

2. **Mosaics** are _____.
   - Ⓐ a flat surface that goes on forever
   - Ⓑ drawings made of shapes
   - Ⓒ designs made out of small pieces of tile
   - Ⓓ designs in a museum

3. How were Escher's tessellations different from the mosaics he saw in Spain?
   - Ⓐ They included things like fish, birds, and lizards.
   - Ⓑ They were made up of geometrical shapes.
   - Ⓒ They used shapes to fill a plane.
   - Ⓓ They included colorful designs.

4. A pattern of shapes that fit together on a plane is called _____.
   - Ⓐ a geometric shape
   - Ⓑ a tessellation
   - Ⓒ a hexagon
   - Ⓓ a triangle

5. How did Escher turn lizards into tessellations?
   - Ⓐ He drew them atop hexagons.
   - Ⓑ He drew them atop squares.
   - Ⓒ He drew them atop triangles.
   - Ⓓ He drew them atop circles.

Bonus: On the back of this page, write four facts about M.C. Escher.

Native American Drumming

Introducing the Topic

1. Reproduce page 135 for individual students, or make a transparency to use with a group or your whole class.

2. Present the drawing of the powwow, and read the caption and labels to connect the new vocabulary with a graphic representation.

Reading the Selection

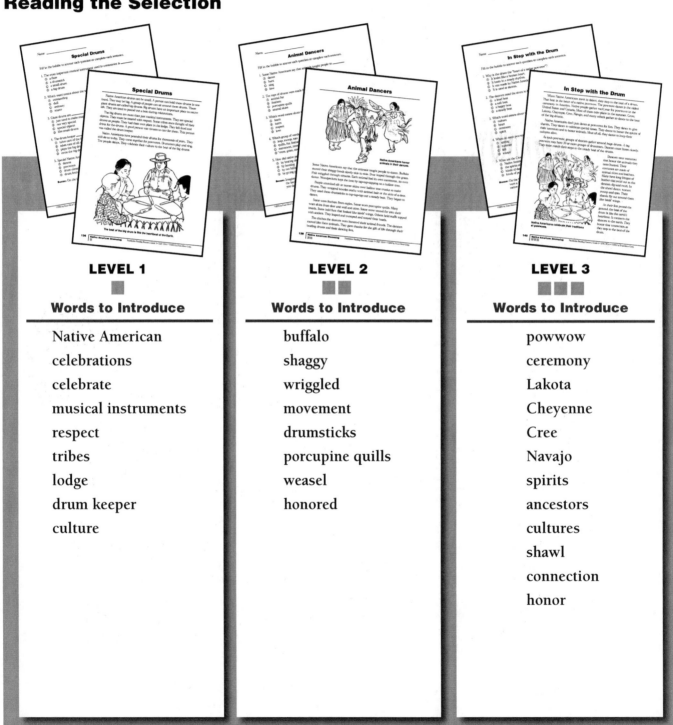

LEVEL 1
■

Words to Introduce

Native American

celebrations

celebrate

musical instruments

respect

tribes

lodge

drum keeper

culture

LEVEL 2
■ ■

Words to Introduce

buffalo

shaggy

wriggled

movement

drumsticks

porcupine quills

weasel

honored

LEVEL 3
■ ■ ■

Words to Introduce

powwow

ceremony

Lakota

Cheyenne

Cree

Navajo

spirits

ancestors

cultures

shawl

connection

honor

Nonfiction Reading Practice, Grade 3 • EMC 3314 • ©2003 by Evan-Moor Corp.

Native American Powwow

dancer

drummer

big drum   drumstick

The big drum keeps the rhythm of the Native American powwow.

Special Drums

Native American drums can be small. A person can hold these drums in one hand. They may be big. A group of people can sit around these drums. These giant drums are called big drums. Big drums have an important place in native life. They are used to pound out a beat during celebrations.

The big drums are more than just musical instruments. They are special objects. They must be treated with respect. Some tribes once thought of their drums as people. They had their own place in the lodge. They left food and drink for the drums. A good person was chosen to care for them. This person was called the drum keeper.

Native Americans have pounded their drums for thousands of years. They still do so today. They come together for powwows. Drummers play and sing. The people dance. They celebrate their culture to the beat of the big drums.

The beat of the big drum is like the heartbeat of the Earth.

Name _____

Special Drums

Fill in the bubble to answer each question or complete each sentence.

1. The most important musical instrument used in ceremonies is _____.
   - Ⓐ a flute
   - Ⓑ a drumstick
   - Ⓒ a small drum
   - Ⓓ a big drum

2. Which word means about the same as **special**?
   - Ⓐ outstanding
   - Ⓑ dull
   - Ⓒ ordinary
   - Ⓓ scarce

3. Giant drums are _____.
   - Ⓐ just used to make music
   - Ⓑ not very special
   - Ⓒ special objects
   - Ⓓ like small drums

4. The drum keeper _____.
   - Ⓐ takes care of the big drum
   - Ⓑ takes care of all of the tribe's drums
   - Ⓒ plays the big drum alone
   - Ⓓ owns the big drum

5. Special Native American ceremonies are called _____.
   - Ⓐ dances
   - Ⓑ powwows
   - Ⓒ drum ceremonies
   - Ⓓ drum festivals

Bonus: On the back of this page, write three facts about the big drum.

Animal Dancers

Native Americans honor animals in their dances.

Some Native Americans say that the animals taught people to dance. Buffalo moved their shaggy heads slowly side to side. Deer leaped through the grass. Fish wriggled through streams. Each animal had its own movement, its own dance. Woodpeckers kept the beat by tap-tap-tapping on a hollow tree.

People stretched elk or moose skins over hollow tree trunks to make drums. They wrapped wooden sticks with animal hair or the skin of a deer. They used these drumsticks to tap-tap-tap out a steady beat. They began to dance.

Some wore feathers from eagles. Some wore porcupine quills. Many wore skins from deer and wolf and otter. Some wove weasel fur into their braids. Some held fans that looked like birds' wings. Others held staffs topped with antlers. They leaped and swooped and tossed their heads.

The clothes the dancers wore honored their animal friends. The dancers moved like these animals. They gave thanks for the gift of life through their beating drums and their dancing feet.

 Nonfiction Reading Practice, Grade 3 • EMC 3314 • ©2003 by Evan-Moor Corp.

Name _____

Animal Dancers

Fill in the bubble to answer each question or complete each sentence.

1. Some Native Americans say that animals taught people to _____.
   - Ⓐ dance
   - Ⓑ hunt
   - Ⓒ sing
   - Ⓓ love

2. The tops of drums were made from _____.
   - Ⓐ animal fur
   - Ⓑ feathers
   - Ⓒ porcupine quills
   - Ⓓ animal skins

3. Which word means about the same as **honor**?
   - Ⓐ learn
   - Ⓑ harm
   - Ⓒ respect
   - Ⓓ love

4. Which group of words relates to costumes native dancers wore?
   - Ⓐ leap, swoop, toss
   - Ⓑ quills, fur, feathers
   - Ⓒ movement, stretch, wriggle
   - Ⓓ trees, grass, streams

5. How did native people give thanks for the gift of life?
   - Ⓐ by beating drums and dancing
   - Ⓑ by hunting
   - Ⓒ by not killing animals
   - Ⓓ by giving presents to each other

Bonus: Imagine that you are a Native American dancer. Choose an animal. On the back of this page, write a sentence telling how you would move if you danced to honor that animal.

In Step with the Drum

When Native Americans meet to dance, they step to the beat of a drum. That beat is the heart of a native powwow. The powwow dance is the oldest ceremony in America. Native people gather each year for powwows in the United States and Canada. Most of them take place in the summer. Crow, Lakota, Cheyenne, Cree, Navajo, and many others gather to dance to the beat of the big drums.

Native Americans don't just dance at powwows for fun. They dance to give thanks. They dance to celebrate special times. They dance to honor the spirits of their ancestors and to honor animals. Most of all, they dance to keep their cultures alive.

At each powwow, groups of dancers gather around huge drums. A big powwow may have 10 or more groups of drummers. Dancers must listen closely. They must match their steps to the steady beat of the drums.

Native Americans celebrate their traditions at powwows.

Dancers wear costumes that honor the animals they once hunted. Their costumes are made of animal skins and feathers. Many have long fringes of leather that swirl out as the dancers dip and twirl. In the shawl dance, women swoop and spin. Their shawls fly out around them like birds' wings.

As their feet pound the ground, the beat of the drum is like the Earth's heartbeat. It connects the dancers to the Earth. They honor that connection as they step to the beat of the drum.

Name _____

In Step with the Drum

Fill in the bubble to answer each question or complete each sentence.

1. Why is the drum the "heart of a native powwow"?
   - Ⓐ It looks like a human heart.
   - Ⓑ It beats in a steady rhythm.
   - Ⓒ It was made by Native Americans.
   - Ⓓ It is used at dances.

2. The dancers need the drum to have _____.
   - Ⓐ a loud beat
   - Ⓑ a soft beat
   - Ⓒ a happy beat
   - Ⓓ a steady beat

3. Which word means about the same as **powwow**?
   - Ⓐ culture
   - Ⓑ heart
   - Ⓒ ceremony
   - Ⓓ spirit

4. When do most powwows take place?
   - Ⓐ spring
   - Ⓑ summer
   - Ⓒ fall
   - Ⓓ winter

5. What are the Crow, Lakota, Cree, and Navajo?
   - Ⓐ Native American tribes
   - Ⓑ the spirits of ancestors
   - Ⓒ kinds of dance costumes
   - Ⓓ kinds of powwows

Bonus: On the back of this page, draw a costume you would like to wear if you were a Native American dancer. Include some of the things you know native dancers use for their costumes.

Faith Ringgold

Introducing the Topic

1. Reproduce page 143 for individual students, or make a transparency to use with a group or your whole class.

2. Present the drawing of the story quilt and artist. Read the caption to connect the new vocabulary with a graphic representation.

Reading the Selection

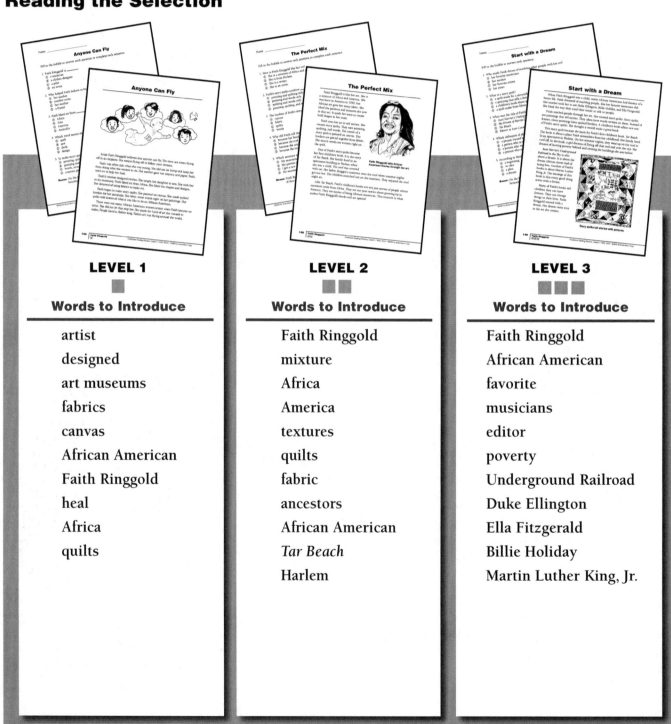

LEVEL 1 ■	**LEVEL 2** ■ ■	**LEVEL 3** ■ ■ ■
Words to Introduce	**Words to Introduce**	**Words to Introduce**
artist	Faith Ringgold	Faith Ringgold
designed	mixture	African American
art museums	Africa	favorite
fabrics	America	musicians
canvas	textures	editor
African American	quilts	poverty
Faith Ringgold	fabric	Underground Railroad
heal	ancestors	Duke Ellington
Africa	African American	Ella Fitzgerald
quilts	*Tar Beach*	Billie Holiday
	Harlem	Martin Luther King, Jr.

Nonfiction Reading Practice, Grade 3 • EMC 3314 • ©2003 by Evan-Moor Corp.

Faith Ringgold, the Artist

This is a type of story quilt. An artist paints a picture on canvas. Quilted borders are added.

Artists learned how to make story quilts from Faith Ringgold.

Anyone Can Fly

Artist Faith Ringgold believes that anyone can fly. She does not mean flying off in an airplane. She means flying off to follow your dreams.

Faith was often sick when she was young. She did not let being sick keep her from doing what she wanted to do. Her mother gave her crayons and paper. Faith used art to help her heal.

Faith's mother designed clothes. She taught her daughter to sew. She took her to art museums. Faith liked art from Africa. She liked the shapes and designs. She dreamed of using fabrics to make art.

Faith began to make story quilts. She painted on canvas. She made quilted borders for her paintings. She often wrote words right on her paintings. Her quilts told stories of what it was like to be an African American.

There were not many African American women artists when Faith became an artist. She did not let that stop her. She made the kind of art she wanted to make. People liked it. Before long, Faith's art was flying around the world.

Nonfiction Reading Practice, Grade 3 • EMC 3314 • ©2003 by Evan-Moor Corp.

Name _____

Anyone Can Fly

Fill in the bubble to answer each question or complete each sentence.

1. Faith Ringgold is _____.
   - Ⓐ a musician
   - Ⓑ a clothes designer
   - Ⓒ a pilot
   - Ⓓ an artist

2. Who helped Faith believe in herself and become an artist?
   - Ⓐ her teacher
   - Ⓑ another artist
   - Ⓒ her mother
   - Ⓓ a friend

3. Faith liked art from _____.
   - Ⓐ Africa
   - Ⓑ Asia
   - Ⓒ America
   - Ⓓ Australia

4. Which word means about the same as **fabric**?
   - Ⓐ quilt
   - Ⓑ sew
   - Ⓒ cloth
   - Ⓓ design

5. To make story quilts, Faith combined _____.
   - Ⓐ painting, quilting, and writing
   - Ⓑ painting and quilting only
   - Ⓒ words, numbers, and pictures
   - Ⓓ crayons, paper, and paint

Bonus: On the back of this page, write a paragraph about what you dream of becoming when you grow up.

The Perfect Mix

Faith Ringgold is like her art. She is a mixture of Africa and America. She was born in America in 1930, but African art gave her many ideas. She liked the patterns and textures she saw in that art. It made her want to create bold shapes in her work.

Faith uses her art to tell stories. She creates story quilts. They mix painting, quilting, and words. The center of a story quilt is painted on canvas. The borders are pieced together from fabric. The story's words are written right on the quilt.

One of Faith's story quilts became her first children's book. It is the story of *Tar Beach.* Her family lived in an apartment building in Harlem when she was a child. The roof was covered with tar. Her father dragged a mattress onto the roof when summer nights got too hot. The children stretched out on the mattress. They enjoyed the cool night air.

Faith Ringgold tells African American stories through her art.

Like *Tar Beach,* Faith's children's books are not just stories of people whose ancestors came from Africa. They are not just stories about growing up in America. They are stories of being African American. This mixture is what makes Faith Ringgold's books and art special.

Nonfiction Reading Practice, Grade 3 • EMC 3314 • ©2003 by Evan-Moor Corp.

Name _____

The Perfect Mix

Fill in the bubble to answer each question or complete each sentence.

1. How is Faith Ringgold like her art?
   - Ⓐ She is a mixture of Africa and America.
   - Ⓑ She is from Harlem.
   - Ⓒ She is a writer.
   - Ⓓ She is an artist.

2. Faith's story quilts combine _____.
   - Ⓐ painting and quilting only
   - Ⓑ painting and words only
   - Ⓒ quilting and words only
   - Ⓓ painting, quilting, and words

3. The borders of Faith's story quilts are pieced together from _____.
   - Ⓐ canvas
   - Ⓑ fabric
   - Ⓒ quilts
   - Ⓓ words

4. *Tar Beach* is the name of Faith Ringgold's first _____.
   - Ⓐ story quilt
   - Ⓑ children's book
   - Ⓒ house in Harlem
   - Ⓓ song about Africa

5. Which sentence uses the word **ancestor** correctly?
   - Ⓐ My ancestors came from Africa.
   - Ⓑ My parents are my ancestors.
   - Ⓒ I got a new bike from my ancestors.
   - Ⓓ My ancestors like me.

Bonus: Faith Ringgold is a mixture of African and American cultures. On the back of this page, write a sentence that tells about your family's cultural background.

Start with a Dream

When Faith Ringgold was a child, many African Americans had dreams of a better life. Faith dreamed of reaching people, like her favorite musicians did. Her mother took her to see Duke Ellington, Billie Holiday, and Ella Fitzgerald. She liked the way they used their music to talk to people.

Faith reached people through her art. She created story quilts. Story quilts are paintings that tell stories. They often have words written on them. Instead of frames, these paintings have quilted borders. A children's book editor saw one of Faith's story quilts. She thought it would make a great book.

This story quilt became the basis for Faith's first children's book, *Tar Beach*. The book is about a place Faith remembers from her childhood. Her family lived in an apartment in Harlem. On hot summer nights, they went up on the roof to cool off. In the book, a girl dreams of flying off that roof and over the city. She dreams of leaving poverty behind and owning the buildings she sees below.

Aunt Harriet's Underground Railroad in the Sky is also about a dream. It is about the dream African slaves had of being free. Another of Faith's books is about Martin Luther King, Jr. The message of this book is that every good thing starts with a dream.

Many of Faith's books tell children that they can have dreams. They can change things in their lives. Faith Ringgold started with a dream. Her dream came true in the art she creates.

Story quilts tell stories with pictures.

Name _____

Start with a Dream

Fill in the bubble to answer each question.

1. Who made Faith dream of reaching other people with her art?
   - Ⓐ her favorite musicians
   - Ⓑ her mother
   - Ⓒ her favorite artists
   - Ⓓ her sister

2. What is a story quilt?
   - Ⓐ a quilt made for a storyteller
   - Ⓑ a painting that tells a story
   - Ⓒ a children's book about quilts
   - Ⓓ a quilt made from fabric

3. What was the title of Faith's first children's book?
   - Ⓐ *Aunt Harriet's Underground Railroad in the Sky*
   - Ⓑ *My Dream of Martin Luther King*
   - Ⓒ *Tar Beach*
   - Ⓓ *Dinner at Aunt Connie's House*

4. Which definition of **slave** best fits the Africans who were <u>not</u> free?
   - Ⓐ a person who is owned by someone else
   - Ⓑ a person who is ruled by a habit
   - Ⓒ a person who works very hard
   - Ⓓ a person who owns someone else

5. According to Martin Luther King, Jr., what does every good thing start with?
   - Ⓐ a beginning
   - Ⓑ an idea
   - Ⓒ a plan
   - Ⓓ a dream

Bonus: On the back of this page, write the title "I Dream." Write a four-line poem beneath the title about your dream for the world.

Walt Disney

Introducing the Topic

1. Reproduce page 151 for individual students, or make a transparency to use with a group or your whole class.

2. Present the animation diagram, and read the caption to connect the new vocabulary with a graphic representation.

Reading the Selection

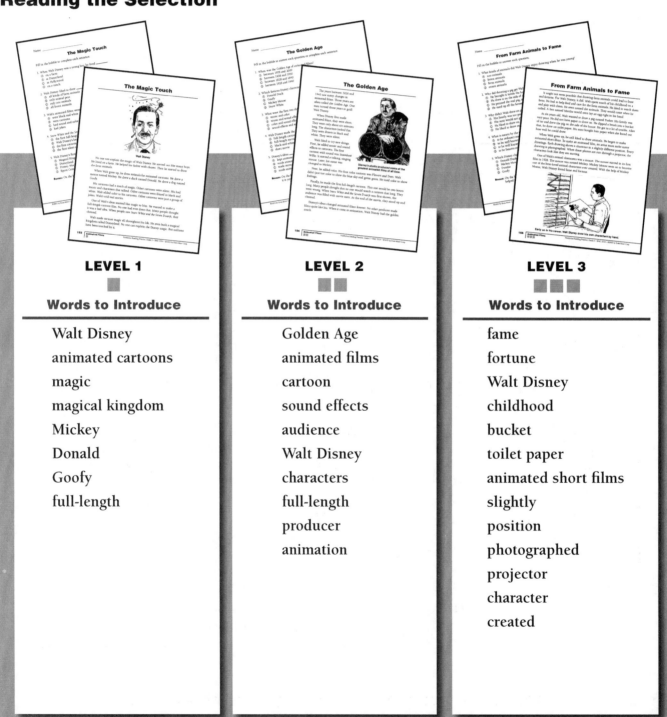

LEVEL 1

Words to Introduce

Walt Disney

animated cartoons

magic

magical kingdom

Mickey

Donald

Goofy

full-length

LEVEL 2

Words to Introduce

Golden Age

animated films

cartoon

sound effects

audience

Walt Disney

characters

full-length

producer

animation

LEVEL 3

Words to Introduce

fame

fortune

Walt Disney

childhood

bucket

toilet paper

animated short films

slightly

position

photographed

projector

character

created

Animation

Animators put together many drawings to create cartoons.

The Magic Touch

Walt Disney

No one can explain the magic of Walt Disney. He started out like many boys. He lived on a farm. He helped his father with chores. Then he started to draw the farm animals.

When Walt grew up, he drew animals for animated cartoons. He drew a mouse named Mickey. He drew a duck named Donald. He drew a dog named Goofy.

His cartoons had a touch of magic. Other cartoons were silent. His had music and characters that talked. Other cartoons were filmed in black and white. Walt added color to his cartoons. Other cartoons were just a group of jokes. Walt's told real stories.

One of Walt's ideas seemed like magic to him. He wanted to make a full-length cartoon film. No one had ever done that. Many people thought it was a bad idea. When people saw *Snow White and the Seven Dwarfs*, they cheered.

Walt made cartoon magic all throughout his life. He even built a magical kingdom called Disneyland. No one can explain the Disney magic. But millions have been touched by it.

   Nonfiction Reading Practice, Grade 3 • EMC 3314 • ©2003 by Evan-Moor Corp.

The Magic Touch

Fill in the bubble to complete each sentence.

1. When Walt Disney was a young boy, he lived _____.
   - Ⓐ on a farm
   - Ⓑ at Disneyland
   - Ⓒ in Hollywood
   - Ⓓ on a ranch

2. Walt Disney liked to draw _____.
   - Ⓐ all kinds of farm animals
   - Ⓑ only animal pets
   - Ⓒ only zoo animals
   - Ⓓ all forest animals

3. Walt's animated films were different because they _____.
   - Ⓐ were black and white
   - Ⓑ were cartoons
   - Ⓒ had sound and color
   - Ⓓ had jokes

4. *Snow White and the Seven Dwarfs* was _____.
   - Ⓐ the first full-length cartoon film
   - Ⓑ Walt Disney's best film
   - Ⓒ the first cartoon in black and white
   - Ⓓ the first silent cartoon film

5. Walt Disney's first magical kingdom was called _____.
   - Ⓐ Magical Kingdom
   - Ⓑ Disneyland
   - Ⓒ Disney World
   - Ⓓ Epcot Center

Bonus: On the back of this page, write four facts about Walt Disney's cartoons.

The Golden Age

The years between 1928 and 1940 saw many changes in animated films. Those years are often called the Golden Age. One man turned those years to gold: Walt Disney.

When Disney first made animated films, they were short. They were only about six minutes long. The characters looked flat. They were drawn in black and white. They were silent.

Walt liked to try new things. First, he added music and sound effects to cartoons. The first cartoon with sound was *Steamboat Willie*. It starred a talking, singing mouse. Later, his name was changed to Mickey.

Disney's studio produced some of the greatest animated films of all time.

Next, he added color. His first color cartoon was *Flowers and Trees*. Walt didn't just use color to show the blue sky and green grass. He used color to show feelings.

Finally, he made the first full-length cartoon. This one would be two hours long. Many people thought that no one would watch a cartoon that long. They were wrong. When *Snow White and the Seven Dwarfs* was first shown, the audience was filled with movie stars. At the end of the movie, they stood up and cheered.

Disney's ideas changed animated films forever. No other producer made films quite like his. When it came to animation, Walt Disney had the golden touch.

Name _____

The Golden Age

Fill in the bubble to answer each question or complete each sentence.

1. When was the Golden Age of animated films?
   Ⓐ between 1978 and 2000
   Ⓑ between 1938 and 1950
   Ⓒ between 1828 and 1840
   Ⓓ between 1928 and 1940

2. Which famous Disney character starred in *Steamboat Willie*?
   Ⓐ Donald Duck
   Ⓑ Goofy
   Ⓒ Mickey Mouse
   Ⓓ Snow White

3. What were the first two things Disney added to his cartoons?
   Ⓐ music and color
   Ⓑ music and sound effects
   Ⓒ color and sound effects
   Ⓓ sound effects and action

4. Walt Disney made the first _____.
   Ⓐ full-length cartoon
   Ⓑ full-length movie
   Ⓒ black-and-white cartoon
   Ⓓ short movie

5. Disney's ideas _____.
   Ⓐ kept animated films the same
   Ⓑ made animated films too long
   Ⓒ made animated films better
   Ⓓ made animated films worse

Bonus: On the back of this page, name your favorite animated film and tell why it is your favorite.

From Farm Animals to Fame

It might not seem possible that drawing farm animals could lead to fame and fortune. For Walt Disney, it did. Walt spent much of his childhood on a farm. He had to help feed and care for the farm animals. He liked to watch them and play with them. He even named the animals. They would come when he called. A hen named Martha would even lay an egg right in his hand.

At six years old, Walt wanted to draw a pig named Porker. His family was very poor. He did not have paper to draw on. He dipped a brush into a bucket of tar and drew the pig on the side of the house. He got in a lot of trouble. After that, he drew on toilet paper. His aunt bought him paper when she found out how well he could draw.

When Walt grew up, he still liked to draw animals. He began to make animated short films. To make an animated film, an artist must make many drawings. Each drawing shows a character in a slightly different position. Every drawing is photographed. When these photos are run through a projector, the characters look like they are moving.

One of Walt's animal characters was a mouse. The mouse starred in its first film in 1928. The mouse was named Mickey. Mickey Mouse went on to become one of the best-loved animal characters ever created. With the help of Mickey Mouse, Walt Disney found fame and fortune.

Early on in his career, Walt Disney drew his own characters by hand.

Nonfiction Reading Practice, Grade 3 • EMC 3314 • ©2003 by Evan-Moor Corp.

Name _____

From Farm Animals to Fame

Fill in the bubble to answer each question.

1. What kinds of animals did Walt Disney enjoy drawing when he was young?
   Ⓐ zoo animals
   Ⓑ forest animals
   Ⓒ farm animals
   Ⓓ ocean animals

2. Why did drawing a pig get Walt into trouble?
   Ⓐ He brought it inside the house to draw it.
   Ⓑ He drew it on the side of the house.
   Ⓒ He painted the real pig, too.
   Ⓓ He used up all the house paint.

3. Why didn't Walt draw on paper when he was very young?
   Ⓐ His family was too poor to buy paper.
   Ⓑ His aunt would not give him any paper.
   Ⓒ He liked to draw on toilet paper.
   Ⓓ He liked to draw on houses.

4. What is meant by the phrase "fame and fortune"?
   Ⓐ to be ordinary and have good luck
   Ⓑ to be well known and have riches
   Ⓒ to be well known and have your future told
   Ⓓ to be famous and well known

5. Which Disney character starred in its first film in 1928?
   Ⓐ Donald Duck
   Ⓑ Mickey Mouse
   Ⓒ Dumbo
   Ⓓ Goofy

Bonus: On the back of this page, write a paragraph telling how farm animals
helped Walt Disney find fame.

Roller Coasters

Introducing the Topic

1. Reproduce page 159 for individual students, or make a transparency to use with a group or your whole class.

2. Present the drawing of the roller coasters, and read the caption and labels to connect the new vocabulary with a graphic representation.

Reading the Selection

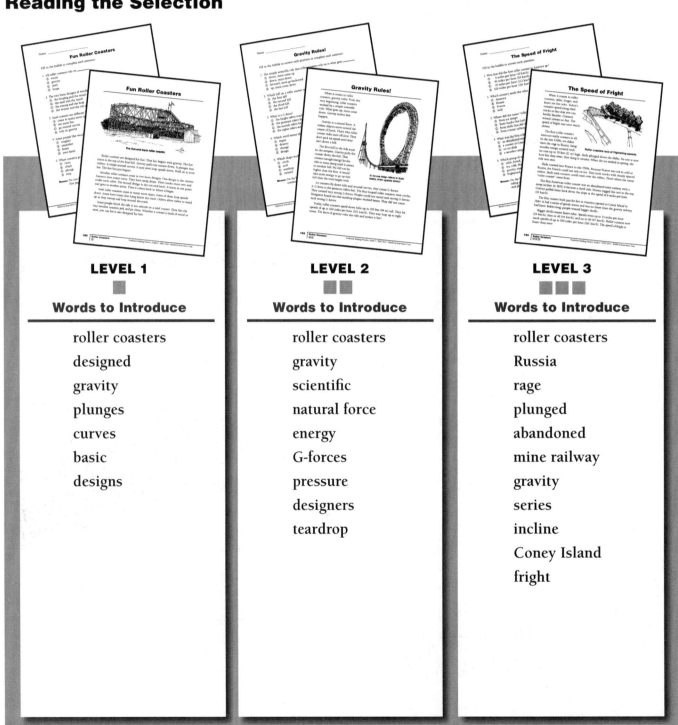

LEVEL 1

Words to Introduce

roller coasters

designed

gravity

plunges

curves

basic

designs

LEVEL 2

Words to Introduce

roller coasters

gravity

scientific

natural force

energy

G-forces

pressure

designers

teardrop

LEVEL 3

Words to Introduce

roller coasters

Russia

rage

plunged

abandoned

mine railway

gravity

series

incline

Coney Island

fright

Roller Coasters

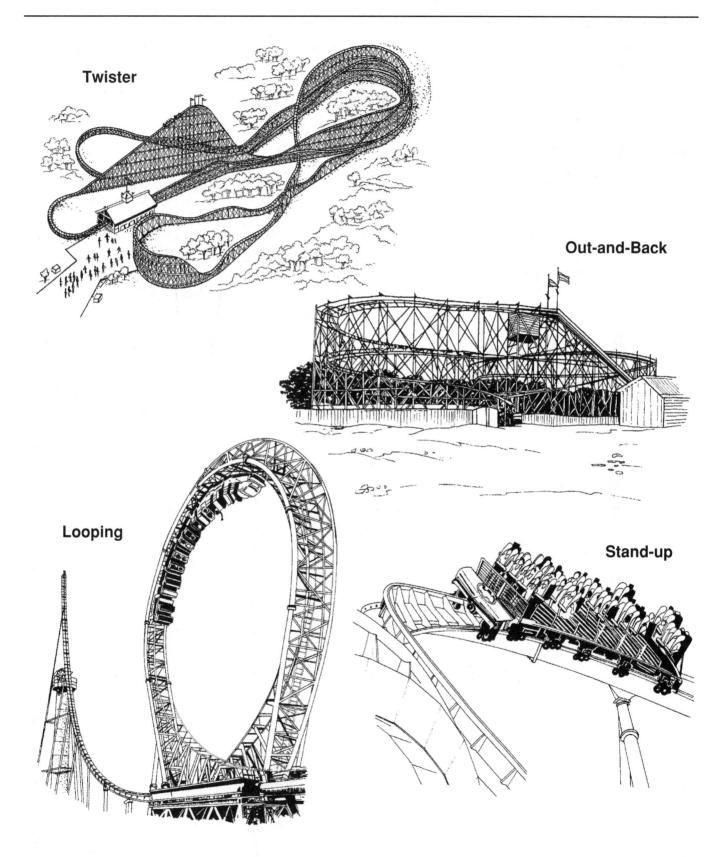

Twister

Out-and-Back

Looping

Stand-up

Roller coasters are designed to be safe, scary, and fun!

Fun Roller Coasters

The out-and-back roller coaster.

Roller coasters are designed for fun! That fun begins with gravity. The fun starts at the top of the first hill. Gravity pulls the coaster down. It plunges into valleys. It whips around curves. It may even loop upside down. Hold on to your hat. The fun has just begun!

Wooden roller coasters come in two basic designs. One design is the twister. Twisters have many turns. They have steep drops. Their tracks cross over and under each other. The second design is the out-and-back. It starts at one point and goes to another point. Then it comes back to where it began.

Steel roller coasters come in many more types. Some of them loop upside down. Some have trains that hang below the track. Others allow riders to stand up as they swoop and loop around the track.

Some people think the ride is too smooth on a steel coaster. They like the way wooden coasters jerk and jar them. Whether a coaster is built of wood or steel, you can bet it was designed for fun!

Nonfiction Reading Practice, Grade 3 • EMC 3314 • ©2003 by Evan-Moor Corp.

Name _____

Fun Roller Coasters

Fill in the bubble to complete each sentence.

1. All roller coasters rely on _____.
   - Ⓐ wood
   - Ⓑ gravity
   - Ⓒ steel
   - Ⓓ loops

2. The two basic designs of wooden coasters are _____.
   - Ⓐ the looping and the stand-up
   - Ⓑ the steel and the wood
   - Ⓒ the swoop and the loop
   - Ⓓ the twister and the out-and-back

3. Steel coasters are different from wooden coasters because they _____.
   - Ⓐ come in many more types
   - Ⓑ are more fun
   - Ⓒ go around curves
   - Ⓓ rely on gravity

4. Some people like wooden coasters better because the ride is _____.
   - Ⓐ rougher
   - Ⓑ smoother
   - Ⓒ faster
   - Ⓓ over quicker

5. When coasters go down steep hills, they _____.
   - Ⓐ twist
   - Ⓑ climb
   - Ⓒ plunge
   - Ⓓ stop

Bonus: Do you like roller coaster rides that are smooth or rough? On the back of this page, give your answer and explain why.

Gravity Rules!

When it comes to roller coasters, gravity rules! From the very beginning, roller coasters worked by a simple scientific rule. What goes up, must come down. Gravity makes that happen.

Gravity is a natural force. It makes objects move toward the center of Earth. That's why roller coaster rides start off slow. They don't pick up speed until they start down a hill.

The first hill in the ride must be the steepest. Gravity pulls the coaster down the hill. That creates enough energy for the ride to coast along until it comes to another hill. No hill can be higher than the first. It would take more energy to go up that hill than the train began with.

G-forces keep riders in their seats, even upside down!

As coasters fly down hills and around curves, they create G-forces. A G-force is the pressure riders feel. The first looped roller coasters were circles. They created very strong G-forces. People could not stand such strong G-forces. Designers found out that teardrop shapes worked better. They did not cause such strong G-forces.

Today, roller coasters speed down hills up to 310 feet (94 m) tall. They hit speeds of up to 100 miles per hour (161 km/h). They may loop up to eight times. The force of gravity rules the ride and makes it fun!

Name _____

Gravity Rules!

Fill in the bubble to answer each question or complete each sentence.

1. The simple scientific rule that roller coasters rely on is what goes _____.
   Ⓐ down, must come up
   Ⓑ down, stays down
   Ⓒ forward, must go backward
   Ⓓ up, must come down

2. Which hill on a roller coaster must be the steepest?
   Ⓐ the first hill
   Ⓑ the second hill
   Ⓒ the third hill
   Ⓓ the last hill

3. What is a G-force?
   Ⓐ the height riders reach
   Ⓑ the pressure riders feel
   Ⓒ the sounds riders hear
   Ⓓ the sights riders see

4. Which word means about the same as **create**?
   Ⓐ repair
   Ⓑ destroy
   Ⓒ change
   Ⓓ design

5. Which shape works best for roller coaster loops?
   Ⓐ circle
   Ⓑ oval
   Ⓒ teardrop
   Ⓓ twisted

Bonus: On the back of this page, write a paragraph that explains how roller
   coasters work.

The Speed of Fright

When it comes to roller coasters, taller, longer, and faster are the rules. Today's coasters speed along their tracks so fast that one can hardly breathe. Coasters weren't always so fast. The speed of fright was once much slower.

Roller coasters race at frightening speeds.

The first roller coasters were not really coasters at all. In the late 1500s, ice slides were the rage in Russia. Steep wooden ramps covered with ice rose up to 70 feet (21 m) high. Sleds plunged down the slides. No one is sure how fast they went. One thing is certain: When the ice melted in spring, the ride was over.

Sleds coasted into France in the 1700s. Because France was not as cold as Russia, the French could not rely on ice. They built tracks with closely spaced rollers. Sleds with runners could coast over the rollers. That's where the name "roller coaster" came from.

The first American roller coaster was an abandoned mine railway with a steep incline. In 1870, it became a thrill ride. Horses tugged the cars to the top. Gravity pulled them back down the slope at the speed of 6 miles per hour (10 km/h).

The first coaster built just for fun in America opened at Coney Island in 1884. It had a series of gentle waves and was no faster than the gravity railway had been. Before long, people wanted bigger thrills.

Bigger thrills meant faster rides. Speeds went up to 15 miles per hour (24 km/h), then to 40 (64 km/h), and on to 60 (97 km/h). Roller coasters in the United States now reach speeds of up to 100 miles per hour (161 km/h). The speed of fright is faster than ever!

Nonfiction Reading Practice, Grade 3 • EMC 3314 • ©2003 by Evan-Moor Corp.

Name _____

The Speed of Fright

Fill in the bubble to answer each question.

1. How fast did the first roller coaster in America go?
   - Ⓐ   6 miles per hour (10 km/h)
   - Ⓑ   40 miles per hour (64 km/h)
   - Ⓒ   70 miles per hour (112 km/h)
   - Ⓓ 100 miles per hour (161 km/h)

2. Which country made the rides that led to today's roller coasters?
   - Ⓐ America
   - Ⓑ Russia
   - Ⓒ France
   - Ⓓ Italy

3. Where did the name "roller coaster" come from?
   - Ⓐ from ice ramps
   - Ⓑ from tracks that had closely spaced rollers
   - Ⓒ from sleds that slid down hills
   - Ⓓ from a mine railway

4. What was the first roller coaster in America?
   - Ⓐ an abandoned mine railway
   - Ⓑ a coaster at Coney Island
   - Ⓒ an ice slide
   - Ⓓ a wooden ramp

5. Which group of words describes the way roller coasters make people feel?
   - Ⓐ calm, bored, sleepy
   - Ⓑ icy, cold, shaken
   - Ⓒ gravity, steep, plunge
   - Ⓓ frightened, thrilled, breathless

Bonus: On the back of this page, write a poem that describes how you feel when riding a roller coaster. Include these vocabulary words: **fright**, **thrill**, **steep**, and **plunge**.

Name _____

A Famous Person

Write the important details about the famous person's life.

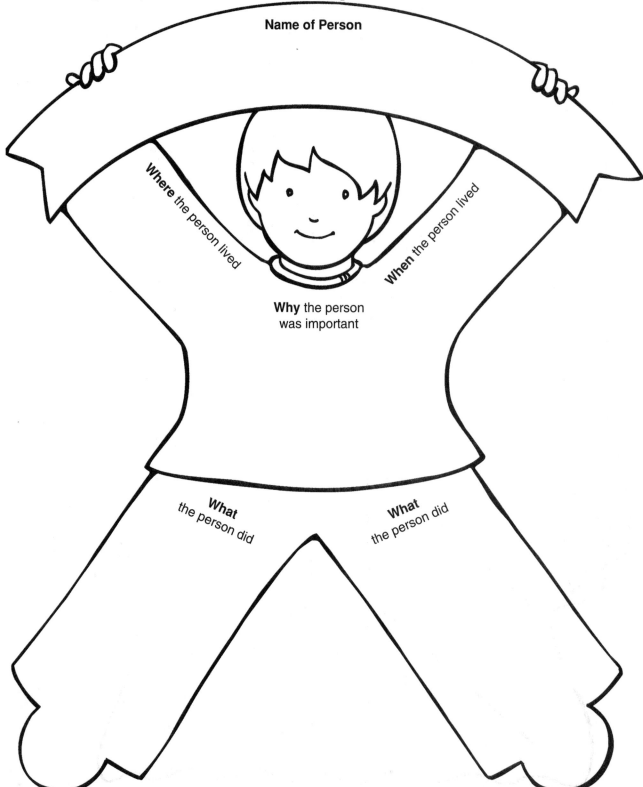

Name of Person

Where the person lived

When the person lived

Why the person was important

What the person did

What the person did

 Nonfiction Reading Practice, Grade 3 • EMC 3314 • ©2003 by Evan-Moor Corp.

Name _____

Fishbone Diagram

Write the main idea of the article on the fish's spine. Write the details between the other bones.

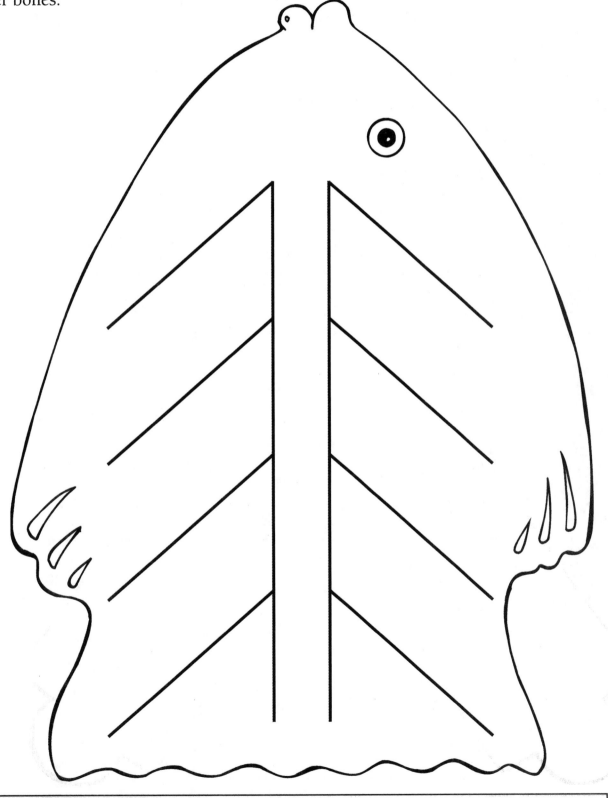

Name _____

Topic

_____

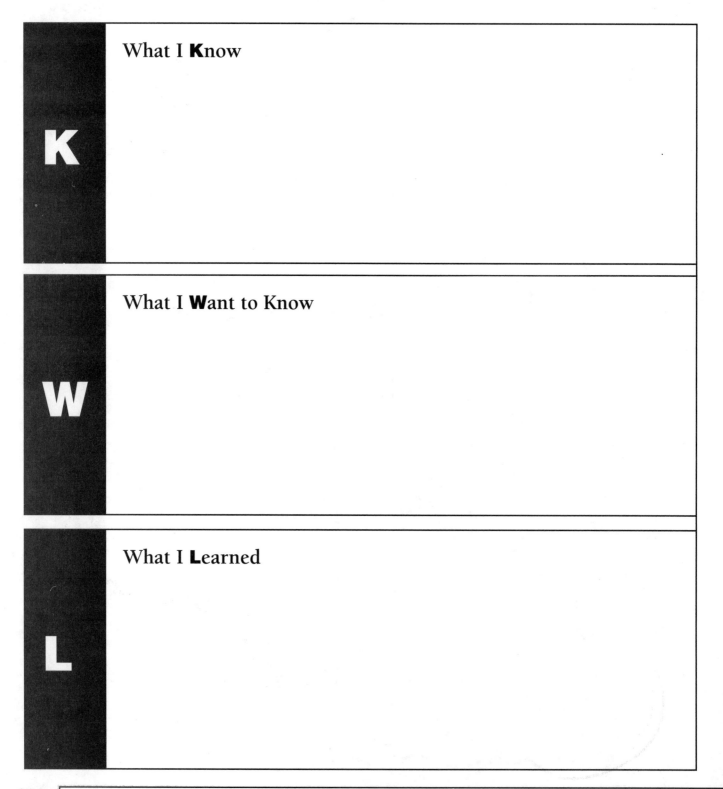

K

What I **K**now

W

What I **W**ant to Know

L

What I **L**earned

Name _____

Sequence Chart

Put the events of the article
in the correct order.

1

2

3

4

5

Name _____

Spider Web

Write the topic of the article in the center of the web. Write details about the topic in the sections of the web.

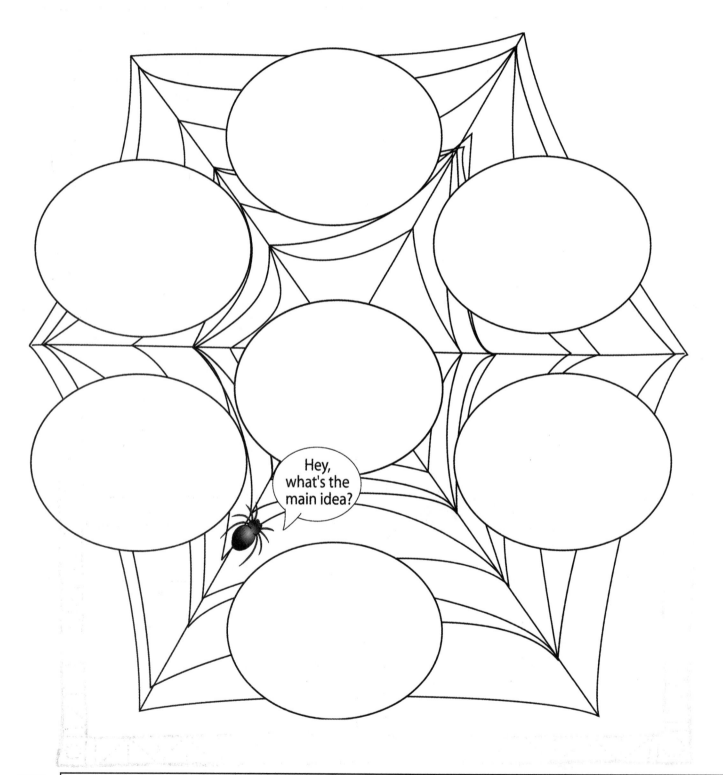

 Nonfiction Reading Practice, Grade 3 • EMC 3314 • ©2003 by Evan-Moor Corp.

Name _____

Word Quilt

Write a new word you have learned in each quilt square. Write or draw what the word means in each quilt square.

Word: _____

Word: _____

Word: _____

Word: _____

Word: _____

Word: _____

Answer Key

page 9
1. A
2. C
3. C
4. B
5. C

Bonus: Answers will vary. Facts given might include: Towers can be made of bricks, wood, stone, or iron. Towers have been built to honor gods and leaders. Towers have been built to show progress. In 1889, the Eiffel Tower was the tallest tower in the world.

page 11
1. D
2. B
3. C
4. D
5. B

Bonus: Answers will vary. Possible responses might include building on soil that is not wet.

page 13
1. C
2. A
3. D
4. B
5. A

Bonus: Answers will vary, but possible responses might include: "I think the tower looks like an ugly, metal chimney." "I think the tower has its own kind of beauty." "I think Eiffel's tower looks very modern."

page 17
1. A
2. C
3. B
4. D
5. C

Bonus: Answers may vary. Statements might include: "Give me freedom, or I will fight." "Let us rule ourselves, or we will fight!"

page 19
1. B
2. B
3. D
4. A
5. C

Bonus: Answers will vary, but might include: "Dear Founding Fathers, Thank you for writing the Constitution." "Dear Founding Fathers, Thank you for making sure one person does not have too much power in the United States."

page 21
1. C
2. B
3. C
4. A
5. D

Bonus: Answers will vary, but should reference that July 4 is Independence Day. Three things might include: fireworks, picnics, and parades.

page 25
1. C
2. B
3. B
4. A
5. D

Bonus: Answers will vary, but might include: "I think Chief Seattle welcomed the white settlers because he thought they were nice." "I think Seattle was a good person." "I think Seattle liked to share." "I think Seattle liked to teach people how to find food and build houses."

page 27
1. A
2. C
3. B
4. A
5. D

Bonus: Answers will vary. Possible responses: Seattle came up with a good plan of attack. His father was chief, so Seattle would take over from him. Seattle was a strong leader that spoke for unity.

page 29
1. A
2. B
3. A
4. A
5. C

Bonus: Answers will vary, but might include: "The land belongs to everyone. I do not want to fight over it. I will sign a treaty, but we both should promise to take care of the land."

page 33
1. C
2. B
3. B
4. C
5. A

Bonus: Answers will vary. Facts given might include: The colonists did not want to pay the tax on tea. The colonists dressed like Indians. The colonists dumped tea into Boston Harbor.

page 35
1. D
2. A
3. C
4. B
5. A
Bonus: Answers will vary, but responses might include protesting homework, cafeteria food, chores, or war.

page 37
1. D
2. B
3. A
4. B
5. C
Bonus: Answers will vary. One possible response: "Friends! Get rid of tea taxes. Come to the Old South Meeting House. Take a stand!"

page 41
1. D
2. B
3. C
4. C
5. B
Bonus: Answers will vary. Animals listed might include: snakes, spiders, fish, monkeys, big cats, macaws, toucans, poison dart frogs, and birds.

page 43
1. C
2. B
3. C
4. D
5. A
Bonus: Answers will vary. One possible response: "I think the rainforest should be saved because it helps us to breathe."

page 45
1. D
2. C
3. A
4. D
5. B
Bonus: Answers will vary. One possible response: "The rainforest canopy is a layer of leaves and branches that covers the forest like a roof. Monkeys, spiders, toucans, jaguars, tapirs, ferns, vines, and leaf litter might be found beneath it."

page 49
1. A
2. B
3. C
4. A
5. D
Bonus: Answers will vary. Facts given might include: Solar winds cause auroras. Auroras appear near Earth's two poles. Auroras are glowing green, red, pink, or purple lights. The glow of an aurora is caused by bits of matter hitting and sparking gases in the sky.

page 51
1. B
2. C
3. A
4. B
5. D
Bonus: Answers will vary, but might include these terms: northern lights, poles, halo, aurora, particles, solar wind, magnetic field, shield, sweep, atoms, collide, oxygen, nitrogen, auroral zone.

page 53
1. B
2. B
3. C
4. A
5. D
Bonus: Answers include: "Two glowing rings formed around the poles of the globe." "He made auroras."

page 57
1. B
2. C
3. A
4. D
5. B
Bonus: Answers will vary. Facts given might include: Poison dart frogs do not hide. They have bright colors. Their bright colors warn other animals to stay away. Eating a poison dart frog can kill an animal. They can be yellow, red, orange, blue, green, or black.

page 59
1. C
2. A
3. C
4. B
5. A
Bonus: Answers will vary. One possible response: "If I were a rainforest hunter, I would pick up the poison dart frog with a leaf so I didn't touch it."

page 61
1. B
2. A
3. C
4. D
5. C
Bonus: Answers will vary. Possible responses include: "Dart frogs make great parents because they stick around." "Dart frogs make great parents because they let their tadpoles hitch a ride on their backs." "Dart frogs make great parents because they carry their tadpoles to pools."

page 65
1. A
2. D
3. B
4. A
5. C
Bonus: Answers will vary. Responses given might include: "They did not have strong enough telescopes to see Pluto. Pluto is very small for a planet. Pluto is at the edge of our solar system."

page 67
1. D
2. B
3. A
4. C
5. A
Bonus: Answers will vary. Responses given might include: "I think astronomers will learn that Pluto is not a planet."

page 69
1. C
2. A
3. B
4. D
5. A
Bonus: Answers will vary. Responses given might include: "I think Pluto is a planet because it orbits the sun." "I don't think Pluto is a planet, because it is like the objects in the Kuiper Belt."

page 73
1. B
2. A
3. B
4. D
5. C
Bonus: Answers will vary. Responses given might include: "I would like a robot to help me do my homework." "I would like a robot to feed my dog."

page 75
1. B
2. A
3. C
4. A
5. C
Bonus: Answers will vary. One possible response: "My robot helper can pick up trash on the beach."

page 77
1. A
2. D
3. A
4. B
5. C
Bonus: Answers will vary. One possible response: "An antbot is like an ant because it has feelers and because it can send out messages to other antbots."

page 81
1. B
2. C
3. D
4. B
5. A
Bonus: Answers will vary. Facts given might include: Chimps live in Africa. Chimps can think and plan. Chimps are a lot like people. Sometimes, chimps fight.

page 83
1. A
2. D
3. D
4. C
5. A
Bonus: Answers will vary, but might include the following: "I would smile and wave." "I would hug the person." "I would shake the person's hand." "I would kiss the person on the cheek."

page 85
1. C
2. A
3. B
4. A
5. D
Bonus: Answers will vary, but might include: "I would like to learn more about wild horses. I want to help save the wild horses so they can be free to gallop on the plains."

page 89
1. B
2. A
3. C
4. B
5. A

Bonus: Answers will vary, but might include: "I will not go to rock concerts." "I will stay away from loud noises." "I will cover my ears."

page 91
1. C
2. D
3. B
4. A
5. B

Bonus: Answers will vary. Sounds listed might include: listening to loud music, going to rock concerts, someone screaming, and a plane taking off.

page 93
1. D
2. A
3. B
4. A
5. C

Bonus: Answers will vary. Possible responses for high sounds—flute, whistle, screech. For low sounds—tuba, foghorn, Dad's voice.

page 97
1. D
2. C
3. A
4. B
5. D

Bonus: Answers will vary, but might include: A safe skater will wear boots that fit. A safe skater will not skate near traffic. A safe skater will wear safety gear.

page 99
1. B
2. D
3. A
4. C
5. A

Bonus: Answers will vary. One possible response: "To get fit, I play basketball."

page 101
1. C
2. B
3. A
4. B
5. D

Bonus: Drawings should show the child wearing a helmet, wrist guards, and elbow and knee pads.

page 105
1. C
2. A
3. B
4. A
5. D

Bonus: Answers will vary. Facts given might include: Edward Jenner wanted to prevent smallpox. Edward Jenner made the first smallpox vaccine. Edward Jenner was a doctor.

page 107
1. B
2. D
3. A
4. B
5. C

Bonus: Answers will vary. One possible response: "Dear Dr. Jenner, Thank you for making the smallpox vaccine. Because of you, kids don't have to worry about getting this scary disease. Your friend, Kim."

page 109
1. A
2. D
3. A
4. B
5. C

Bonus: Answers will vary. Facts given might include: Smallpox causes high fever, body aches, and sores. Smallpox can kill you. Smallpox can leave bad scars. A vaccine can prevent smallpox.

page 113
1. C
2. A
3. A
4. B
5. D

Bonus: Answers will vary. One possible interpretation: "My favorite kind of race is a bicycle race."

page 115
1. D
2. A
3. B
4. B
5. C

Bonus: Answers will vary, but might include the following: I would like to be Mike Marsh because I like to run. I would like to be Bob Beamon because I like to jump. I would like to be Simon Ammann because I like to ski.

page 117
1. B
2. C
3. A
4. B
5. C
Bonus: Answers will vary. An example of one math problem might be: Which country won the fewest number of medals? Answer: Sweden

page 121
1. C
2. D
3. B
4. A
5. C
Bonus: Answers will vary, but might include: "December 25 is most important to me because it is Christmas." "[Dates will vary] is most important to me because it is my birthday."

page 123
1. C
2. A
3. A
4. C
5. A
Bonus: Answers will vary, but might include the following: People needed calendars to help them know when to plant. The first calendars followed cycles of the moon. Egyptian calendars were based on the sun. Today's calendars are based on the sun.

page 125
1. D
2. A
3. A
4. C
5. D
Bonus: Answers will vary. One possible response: "My favorite holiday is Christmas. If it fell in the wrong season, there might be flowers blooming. There might not be any snow to build a snowman. We could not bundle up and sing carols."

page 129
1. A
2. B
3. D
4. C
5. A
Bonus: Answers will vary, but should include math concepts like measuring, counting, and matching shapes.

page 131
1. D
2. B
3. A
4. B
5. C
Bonus: Answers will vary. Facts given might include: Tiling is the art of using shapes to cover a plane. Squares, triangles, and hexagons are shapes that can be used separately to tile a plane. Artists use tilings on pottery, wood carvings, and stained glass.

page 133
1. D
2. C
3. A
4. B
5. A
Bonus: Answers will vary, but might include the following: M.C. Escher was not good at math when he was a boy. M.C. Escher used tessellations to make art. M.C. Escher understood the math of shapes.

page 137
1. D
2. A
3. C
4. A
5. B
Bonus: Answers will vary. Facts given might include: A group of people can sit around the big drum. The big drum is a sacred object. A drum keeper takes care of the big drum. Native Americans play the big drum at powwows.

page 139
1. A
2. D
3. C
4. B
5. A
Bonus: Answers will vary, but might include: "If I danced to honor a buffalo, I would shake my head slowly side to side." "If I danced to honor a fish, I would wriggle."

page 141
1. B
2. D
3. C
4. B
5. A
Bonus: Drawings will vary. Elements of native costuming to look for include the following: animal skins, feathers, leather fringes, shawls (for girls).